651.78

EXECUTIVE WRITING
Plain English at work

Pitman

PITMAN PUBLISHING
128 Long Acre, London WC2E 9AN

A Division of Longman Group UK Limited

First published in Great Britain 1991

British Library Cataloguing in Publication Data

Murphy, Elizabeth M.
   Effective writing: plain English at work.
   1. English language. Business English. Writing skills
   I. Title   II. Snell, Shelagh
   808.066651021

ISBN 0 273 03482 0

Designed by Lisa Lambert

Printed and bound in Singapore

Preface

I have written this book in response to requests from participants in my courses in effective writing in public and private offices, and in colleges and universities. My aim has been to provide the basis of skills needed for:
• improving writing skills in a multi-skilled work environment,
• understanding how to make writing make more sense,
• learning how to explain plain English to others, and
• getting rid of gobbledegook in all official writing.
I want to thank all the people who have contributed to this book by being participants in my courses — your ideas helped me a lot. This book is for you.

Elizabeth M Murphy
Canberra, 1989

Contents

Introduction

The purpose of writing is to communicate — at least two people are involved: a writer and a reader. The writer's aim is to get a message across to a reader with as little effort on the reader's part as possible. The best way to write effectively is to use correct, plain English. This means having a firm grasp of grammar, spelling and punctuation; and it means using words and structures that you are comfortable with because you use them every day in speech. Writing is an art. Very few people are born writers — we all have to learn how to do it effectively. The good news is that you can learn, and it's never too late.

This book is about plain English in the workplace; that is, it is about writing working documents effectively. By working documents I mean those documents that have to do a job for you, such as minutes, memos, letters and reports. It is not a cookbook of formulas for writing these documents: rather it is a guide to putting together sentences and paragraphs so that they will be as plain as possible. You can then apply what you learn to any documents you have to write — pamphlets, forms, speeches and reports, as well as theses, articles and even stories — and be sure that you are getting your message across.

How to use this book

If you are using this book as a self tutor, you may find you need to consult a full grammar text to follow up some points, or your own office style manual for particular style variations. If you are using it as a course workbook, your tutor may skip some bits and may give extra exercises in other places, depending on the level you have reached. But whichever way you are working, there are many exercises for you to practise on. You (or your tutor) pick and choose the exercises which will be most helpful to you. For example, if you find you are having difficulty with one point of grammar or style in your writing, you may choose to do all the exercises on that point instead of just a few. However, as the book proceeds logically from the smallest units of writing (words) to the largest (whole documents), it is best if you also proceed through it in the order in which it is arranged.

The pattern of most of the sections is:

$$\text{theory + examples} \longrightarrow \text{exercises} \longrightarrow \text{solutions}$$

Solutions (or suggested solutions), when applicable, appear immediately after exercises. They are printed in smaller type and are enclosed in a box.

When you see these boxed solutions, cover them up and try to do the exercises on your own. If you have difficulty with any exercise, go back and revise the whole section before trying the exercise again.

1 What is effective writing?

Effective writing is writing that works. It does its job without anyone having to ask for further explanation. If it informs, it does so clearly — the reader does not have to ask for more information. If it replies to a question or a request, it does so fully — all the reader's points are dealt with in one way or another. If it asks for information, it gives the reader sufficient background and asks understandable questions so that the correct information will be elicited.

Effective writing at work gets its message through quickly, economically, clearly and correctly. Workers at all levels are busy people and do not have time to decipher unclear messages, cope with poor grammar or spelling, or look up dictionary meanings of obscure expressions.

What to avoid

We have all had to try and read a document that is not clear. What made it unclear? There are many causes — here are a few that people usually quote:

- consistently poor spelling
- insufficient or incorrect punctuation
- poor proofreading
- long, involved or incomplete sentences
- illogical paragraphing and poor internal paragraph structure
- misuse of parts of speech, such as using adjectives for adverbs
- ambiguity
- not getting to the point
- overuse of passive verbs
- mixing tenses of verbs
- use of clichés, buzz-words and jargon without explanation
- insufficient or incorrect information

Here is an example of an ineffective memorandum followed by an effective memorandum on the same subject:

Memorandum

TO   All staff

FROM   Staff Development Director

DATE   18 July 19- -

SUBJECT EFFECTIVE WRITING WORKSHOP

A workshop will be held in J-6 next Monday and Tuesday for staff. To help you develop writing skills.

Typists, filing clerks and field supervisors who feel the necessity to up-grade said skills are hereby encouraged to see that an application is submitted to be considered for inclusion. Or anyone else.

The procedural practices concerning the writing of memorandums and simple reports will be learned if advantage is taken of this opportunity by phoning my secretary before c.o.b. on Wednesday, however you must hurry due to the fact that only 22 places exist.

P Jones

Memorandum

TO   All staff

FROM   Staff Development Director

DATE   18 July 19- -

SUBJECT EFFECTIVE WRITING WORKSHOP

A Workshop on Effective Writing will be held in the training room next Monday and Tuesday from 9 am to 5 pm.

2 The purpose of this presentation is to help staff who do not normally write documents themselves to develop their writing skills. Target groups include typists, filing clerks, field supervisors and any others who would like to take advantage of the opportunity. I hope that, as a result, many of you will feel more confident about writing simple documents such as memorandums and short reports.

3 If you would like to participate in the workshop, please phone my secretary, Lyn, on extension 3456, before 5 pm on Wednesday. There is a limit of 22 places on the workshop, so act promptly if you are interested.

P Jones

Compare these two memorandums. Why is the first one ineffective? Why is the second one more effective? You may notice that the first has several of the faults mentioned in the list above. The whole purpose of this book, in fact, is to explain how they differ. To begin answering these questions, and to outline the principles of effective writing, we need to look at the background of communication.

Writing is communication — how does it work?

Writing is a means of communication. For communication to occur at all, there has to be:

- an *idea*
- a reason for wanting to pass the idea on — a *purpose*
- a *means* of doing so (for example, writing),
- actual *encoding* (writing) the message, and
- the *sending* of the message.

These are the responsibilities of the *sender* of the message. But communication is not complete until a *receiver* has received and understood it. So the receiver:

- *receives* the message, and
- *decodes* it (that is, understands the writing if writing is the code used).

So far, so good; but the sender still does not know that the receiver has got the message correctly, if at all. There has to be feedback to complete the communication cycle. The receiver has to *respond*.

The Communication Cycle

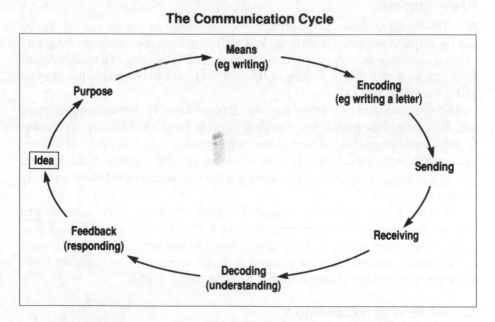

If the response is what the sender expected, the communication has been **effective**. For example:

- *Sender* issues instructions for the factory to close at 3 pm
- *Response:* factory knock-off whistle blows at 3 pm

- *Sender* asks for a particular file
- *Response:* the file duly appears on the sender's desk

If the response is not what the sender expected, communication is **ineffective**: the communication cycle has broken down somewhere. For example:

- *Sender* writes guidelines to go with a complicated form
- *Response:* public constantly phone to seek clarification. *Possible cause:* language of form and/or guidelines too complex for general public users

Communication breakdown can be avoided by making sure that you:

- stick to one **topic** whenever possible — if you really must write about two topics in the one letter, for example, label them clearly with appropriate subject and side headings;
- keep your **purpose** in mind while writing — be clear whether you are writing to inform or to get information;
- make sure that both you and your reader understand the **relevance** of the document — where it fits in a wider social context or into a set of similar documents, for example;
- consider the **audience** who will read/use the document — who they are, what they know, what you want them to know or do;
- use **language** which is appropriate to the audience, the purpose and the topic;
- package your document attractively and professionally (see chapter 11).

Plain English

Now that we have looked at the principles of communication, we can expand on our description of effective writing. It is writing which uses the right language to get its message across, and which gets the correct response. To a large extent your attitude to the task of writing will be determined by how much thought you give to the principles above.

The actual success of your writing will depend, however, on the language you use. Be aware of the principles of writing in **plain English**. Nobody in business or public administration has time to wade through English which would be better in an eighteenth century novel, if anywhere at all, and nobody in the general public will bother to read even a pamphlet if the first sentence is less than totally plain.

What is 'plain' English? It is standard English which is *correct* according to present-day standards of grammatical correctness; it is *clear*, expressing precisely what you mean as concisely as possible; and it is *appropriate* for the topic and audience concerned — for instance, it would use simpler vocabulary if the audience consisted of children than if it consisted of adults.

Grammar and expression

This book does not go into the fine details of grammar — there are many other grammar textbooks available that do this. However this book does review some of the more basic general principles of grammar that are essential if you want to be understood at all. When people write business documents to each other, they first have to use words, sentence structures and punctuation that each understands. They also have to conform to a particular level of English that is the one used for business communication. If a writer uses a form of the language that the reader does not associate with business, there is a breakdown in communication. Business writing is less stilted now than even a few years ago — many informal expressions are acceptable now in even quite formal documents. The rule is that writing should be as natural as possible while avoiding substandard expressions (slang, vulgarisms, pomposity etc). Use words you are comfortable with, that you would use in conversation, but make sure they are put together according to the accepted patterns of standard English grammar.

Style

Correct grammar alone will not ensure that a sentence works. Some very long sentences are grammatically correct, but they fail because they are very long. Some sentences seem readable until we strike a word or expression that seems to jar or conflict with the structure of the rest of the sentence. The writer's aim should be to be understood at first reading. It is your responsibility to be clear — not your reader's to unscramble your muddled message. Whatever your purpose, to be clear you need to make sure you do not confuse your reader by writing:

- sentences that jar because of inconsistent structure (non-parallelism),
- sentences that could have two meanings (ambiguity), or
- sentences that leave the reader in mid-air (fragments).

There are some extra aspects of writing that you need to be aware of when you write documents that must do a job as quickly and efficiently as possible. These include:

- length of sentences,
- active or passive verbs,
- dynamism — action verbs or verbal nouns,
- appropriate words for the occasion and the audience,
- economy of words,
- jargon — avoid or explain.(See chapters 9-10.)

Beyond the writing

Often a document can be written in English that is impeccably correct and entirely appropriate stylistically for the purpose and the target audience, yet fail. Why?

Have you ever opened a pamphlet in search of a quick answer and found yourself ploughing through a sea of unrelieved black type? Have you ever tried to read a report with numbered paragraphs and wondered which 'decimal place' this paragraph was the sub-sub-section of? Have you ever tried to make sense of a paragraph of confusing statistics that would have been as plain as day in tabular or graphic form?

These, and other similar problems are the fault of bad design. The way the information is presented to the reader is as much the writer's responsibility as grammar is.

This does not mean that you have to become an ace designer. It does mean, however, that you have to think of the visual impact of your words and the way they appear on the page. You have to consider such things as:

- Logical paragraphing
- Use of white space
- Use of facilities available on modern typewriters, word processors and computers (such as different typefaces, bold type, italics etc)
- Signalling new information — graded headings, numbering etc
- Use of graphic means of giving information (especially statistics)

All the points outlined above, and many more, will be discussed in this book. When you have worked through it, either on your own or in a course with a tutor, you will be equipped to write effectively. It does not provide you with magic formulas for writing every document you might ever need to write. It gives you the basic knowledge you need to write effectively, and some examples of the more common documents — it is up to you to put the principles into practice in every document you write from now on.

2 Correct writing

Primarily, effective writing is correct writing. How do we know whether our writing is correct or not? We know by knowing whether or not we have followed the rules for correct writing in the standard form of English.

It is difficult to talk about what is or is not correct if we do not know the terms that are used to describe the many areas of writing. You probably learned some of these terms at school — do *noun, verb, phrase, clause, active, passive* ring any bells with you? Whether you left school last year or a long time ago, you may have forgotten these terms, so this part of the book is designed to remind you. Skip it if it is all familiar to you.

Some participants in courses ask: Why do I have to know these terms? Can't I just learn to write?

If you learn to be a doctor or a lawyer, a plumber or a salesperson, you learn the terms that everyone in that profession or trade uses. You are learning to develop your writing skills, so you need to control some of the terms that are used in the writing business. You need to understand the language of writing so that we can discuss it together.

Writing consists of strings of words, broken up by punctuation marks, and arranged in chunks of several lines each. If you don't conform to a writing pattern that your readers will understand, you cause confusion. This confusion may take the form of hesitation, a need to re-read a passage, or doubt about the meaning of a group of words. When you write in a confused style, your readers have to ask for clarification; supervisors tell you to write it again because it 'doesn't make sense'.

How do you know what to correct if you are told that your writing 'doesn't make sense'? If you are a supervisor, how do you explain to the writer exactly what is causing the confusion in the document? The only way is to use the terminology of grammar or of style. You can then be precise. If it's a grammar problem, for instance, you can say: 'This sentence is confused because the verb doesn't agree with the subject' or 'It would flow better if we used commas between the clauses instead of all these conjunctions'.

The early chapters in this book are about essential grammar. There are not many terms to understand, and you should not memorise mere definitions. It is more important to get a feel for how nouns differ from verbs, when to use adverbs and when to use adjectives, which punctuation marks to use where, and so on. If you can do this, you will be on the way to understanding the difference between good and bad writing, and that understanding will certainly help you to write better, and help you to help others to write better.

A quick skim of this section may be all you need to bring the terms and the functions of the various parts of the sentence to mind. Or you may wish to work right through, completing all the exercises along the way. If you make a lot of mistakes in an exercise, perhaps you should revise the whole section or consult a full grammar text. It is not a good idea to skip over something you haven't fully understood. When you have completed the section, you should be more confident that your writing will be grammatically acceptable.

Theory is kept to a minimum — indeed, there is only as much of it as is necessary to remind you of the terms and of how words work in the most straightforward of sentences.

After this exercise, let us start by looking at spelling, parts of speech and sentence structure.

Grammar pre-test

Here is an exercise that you can try as a pre-test of your knowledge and competence in each of these areas.

Part A Parts of Speech
1 Underline the *nouns* in the following sentences:
   eg <u>Jack</u> and <u>Jill</u> went up the <u>hill</u>.
   (a) The jury at the trial in Birmingham is still considering its verdict.
   (b) My canary is an excellent whistler.
2 Underline the *pronouns* in the following sentences:
   (a) He made himself a cup of coffee and then left it on the window ledge.
   (b) These are the books I need, but I don't need those over there.
3 Underline the *verbs* (or *verb phrases* — that is, verbs consisting of more than one word) in the following sentences:
   If you can, also label each as *active* (A) or *passive* (P).
   (a) He read the label carefully as he had been caught by misleading labels before.
   (b) Unless you have enrolled as a full-time student, you will not be given a grant.
4 Underline the *adjective* (or *adjective phrases* — that is, adjectives consisting of more than one word) in the following sentences. If you can, also label each as *positive* (P), *comparative* (C) or *superlative* (S):
   (a) This beautiful rose is the prettiest in my garden which is newer than yours.
   (b) His report was the shortest I received, although he was very slow preparing it.
5 Underline the *adverbs* in the following sentences:
   (a) Ann works quietly and efficiently, but nobody works more quickly than Peter.
   (b) They are very happy to be home and quite content to live quietly now.

6 Underline the *prepositions* in the following sentences. If you can, also draw a circle around **one** whole *prepositional phrase.*
  (a) The customer in the blue raincoat bought the picture of the old English village.
  (b) Under this building is a secret passage leading into the bank next door.
7 Underline the *conjunctions* in the following sentences:
  (a) Although it rained, we enjoyed our picnic because we are all good friends.
  (b) Your essay is not marked yet, but it will be ready tomorrow or the next day.

Part B   Sentences or fragments
Say whether the groups of words that follow are whole *sentences* (S) or only *fragments* (F) (incomplete as sentences in some way). If there are any *fragments*, **add** to the beginning or end whatever words are necessary to make them into complete *sentences*. Do not alter the wording of the original groups of words.

1 Although it rained
2 Despite the length of the journey and the number of people she had to see on the way
3 If only you had told me yesterday
4 Please shut the door
5 Before I went out into the freezing cold of the winter day where I could see through the window that the garden was covered with frost

Part C   Check of some areas of spelling and grammar
There are several errors in each of these sentences. Make all necessary corrections. Do not alter words or word order unless necessary.

1 Its bad manners to except an invitation when your all ready commited to another function.
2 After trying in vain to contact you by phone, this letter will confirm your appointment as head of the english department.
3 The ladies' shoe department is on the first floor and the mens' are on the second floor.
4 When he announced the name of the winner so quickly, it supprised everyone.

There are no marks for this grammar test, but you could note how many errors you made in the whole test. Later, there will be another test for you to try. You could compare your results.

Solutions to Grammar Pre-test

Part A
1   (a) jury, trial, Birmingham, verdict; (b) canary, whistler
2   (a) He, himself, it; (b) These, I, I, those
3   (a) read [A], had been caught [P]; (b) have enrolled [A], will not be given [P]
4   (a) beautiful [P], prettiest [S], newer [C]; (b) shortest [S], slow [P]
5   (a) quietly, efficiently, more quickly; (b) very, quite, quietly, now
6   (a) in [in the blue raincoat], of [of the old English village]; (b) under [under this building], into [into the bank next door]
7   (a) although, because; (b) but, or

Part B

1 F: ... , we still went for a walk.

2 F: ... , she was not tired.

3 F: ..., I could have helped you.

4 S

5 F ..., I put on an extra pullover.

Part C

1 It's bad manners to accept an invitation when you're already committed to another function.

2 As I have been unable to contact you by phone, I am writing to confirm your appointment as head of the English department.

3 The ladies' shoe department is on the first floor and the men's [shoe department] is on the second floor.

4 (a) Everyone was surprised at the speed with which the winner's name was announced.
   OR
   (b) The name of the winner, which he announced quickly, was a surprise to everyone.

3 Spelling

Poor spelling is one of the characteristics of poor writing. It defeats the purpose of words, which is to communicate meaning. It annoys readers and it is avoidable. Here are some hints for helping you to spell better than you do.

Use your dictionary

Never guess at the spelling of a word if you know that you are a poor speller. Become familiar with the format of your dictionary and what you can learn from it besides mere spellings and definitions. Some people who are very bad at spelling complain 'How can I use a dictionary when I don't know what letter the word begins with?' Take a word like *photograph*. If you hear it for the first time, how do you know whether it begins with *f* or *ph*? Both have the same sound in English. Or take a word like *through*. Is that spelled *threw, throo, thrwo, throu,* or *through*? There are words in English in which the *oo* sound is represented by each of these spellings.

For fun, try to decipher this sentence. It is spelled using letter combinations which give sounds like the correct ones:

Thairs ghyti phoor lounch.

Solution

Thairs	= there's	
ghyti	= fish	**gh** = **f** (as in enou<u>gh</u>)
		y = **i** (as in p<u>y</u>ramid)
		ti = **sh** (as in na<u>ti</u>on)
phoor	= for	**ph** = **f** (as in <u>ph</u>oto)
		oor = **or** (as in p<u>oor</u>)
lounch	= lunch	**ou** = **u** (as in y<u>ou</u>ng)

Is it any wonder that many people find some English spelling difficult?

My advice to poor spellers is to write the word down, spelling it all possible ways and then check for the correct spelling in the dictionary. English spelling comes from a history of involvement with many languages, so you will find a study of the origin of a word will help you with the spelling of that word and many others from the same source.

Read carefully

As you read anything — dictionary, novel, business letter — make a mental note of any new words you find. Practise using them and practise using their derivatives. For example, if you see the word *democratise* for the first time, think about its origin — *democracy* (noun) from the Greek words for *people* and *strength*. Can we make *democratisation* from that? Yes, although it is now a rather unwieldy word. Think of other derivatives. Learn as much as you can about words that are new to you.

Memorise groups of words

You may have noticed that *democratise* ended in *-ise* (in some countries, it is *-ize*). There are times when it pays to learn families of verb endings, for example, *advise, practise, license* and so on. In this instance, the *-se* ending distinguishes the verbs from their noun counterparts — *advice, practice, licence*.

There are other groups of words you can learn such as: confusing words — *lay, lie* and all their tenses; words from similar sources such as *emigrate, immigrate*; or words that look similar but have totally different meanings such as *dessert, desert*. There are many hundreds more. Often the only way to remember their spellings is to memorise them in groups along with their meanings.

Analyse unknown words

Remember that words in English come from a number of sources and have been used to make new words by adding on to these existing words. This knowledge helps with spelling. When you come across a new word that has several parts, break it up into its parts. For example, take the word *mismanagement*. This can be broken up into the prefix *mis-*, the root word *manage* and the suffix *-ment* . You know how to spell *-mis* and *-ment* because they appear so often. The only part left to learn is *manage* and that is now easy. Even very long words can be broken up like this. Here is one that is said to be one of the longest in the English language:

antidisestablishmentarianism

Spelling this could be a daunting task, but it becomes easy when you break it up into all its prefixes and suffixes:

anti - dis - establish - ment - arian - ism

Just spelling a word is not enough, of course. As you spell a word, try to understand its meaning. Even a very long word becomes meaningful when you break it up and realise that its meaning is the sum of the meanings of all its parts.

Make lists of troublesome words

There are some words which cause trouble to nearly everyone. We have already seen that there can be confusion in the use of the verbs *lay* and *lie*. Others are *affect/effect*, *eminent/imminent*, *stationary/stationery* and there are hundreds more. I recommend that you keep a small notebook to write down any pairs or groups of words that confuse you, and the different meanings each has; also record any words that are unusual or difficult in any way. However, just listing words will not help you to learn them — refer to your list as often as possible, and try to use the words in an appropriate context whenever you have an opportunity. Unused words, like unused machinery, get rusty.

Follow the rules of spelling

There are some rules that can help you. If you try to understand them, the exceptions will then be easier to remember. Below I have summarised some of the most troublesome spelling rules, with just a couple of examples and exceptions to each.

Rule	Examples	Exceptions (some only)
IE / EI		
I before E except after C, but only when the sound is 'EE' as in 'need'	achieve believe shield	seize weird
(Pronounce the following as you read them, and note that they do not contain the 'EE' sound: neighbour, friend, height, foreign They are therefore not governed by this rule.)	deceive receipt ceiling	
Final silent E		
Drop before endings that begin with a vowel like *-ing, -ed, -ous -er, -en*	wipe/wiping taste/tasted fame/famous joke/joker take/taken	(Retain E after soft C and soft G before suffix beginning with A or O:) noticeable, manageable, advantageous.
Keep before ending that begins with a consonant like *-ly*	polite/ politely	
Final Y		
Change Y to I if preceded by a consonant and followed by any ending except one that begins with I.	beauty beautiful BUT hurry hurrying	dry dryness sly slyness (BUT ugly ugliness)
Keep the Y if preceded by a vowel	valley valleys	day daily pay paid say said (Did you notice that the root words here are one-syllable words?)

Rule	Examples	Exceptions (some only)
Double the final consonant		
When adding -ed, -er, -est, -ing to a final consonant with a single vowel before it.	drop/dropped beg/begging fat/fatter thin/thinnest	Final consonant is NOT doubled if: • word ends with two consonants: farm/farmer • final consonant is preceded by two vowels: beat/beating
When the consonant is at the end of a word of more than one syllable, where the stress is on the last syllable of the root word	omit/omitted transfer/ transferred/ transferral	Final consonant is not doubled if stress is on other than the last syllable: *differ/differing* (but note transference)
Double the final L		
If there is one vowel before it but not if there are two vowels before it , with endings -ed, -ing, -er	pedal/pedalled BUT feel/feeling	parallel/paralleled
Add K to words ending in C		
Before ending that begins with E or I	picnic picnicking picnicked	
-CEDE -CEED -SEDE		
Except for *supersede, exceed, proceed, succeed,* all words that have this sound end in -CEDE	accede concede precede	

Plurals of nouns

Most nouns form the plural by adding -s to the singular, as in *book/books*.

Words ending in o, s, x, ch, sh or z form the plural by adding -es, as in *echo/echoes, boss/bosses, box/boxes, buzz/buzzes*.

Words ending in y change y to ie and add -s, if the y is preceded by a consonant: *sky/skies, city/cities*. If it is preceded by a vowel, it simply adds -s:*monkey/monkeys*.

The plural of most words ending in f is -ves, as in *loaf/loaves, thief/thieves*. Exceptions are: *roof/roofs, chief/chiefs*.

There are many irregular plural endings which cause spelling problems. A few are given here:

- ox/oxen
- deer/deer
- mouse/mice
- plateau/plateaux
- criterion/criteria

- datum/data (but data is now used in singular sense too.)

Use your dictionary if you are not sure.

Note: Do not use apostrophe *s* to indicate plural. There is a modern and quite incorrect tendency to write, for example, *onion's* to mean more than one onion. Apostrophe *s* is only ever used for the plural where a final s without an apostrophe would be confusing, as in: Dot your is (*Dot your i's*).

Plurals of compounds

Plurals of compounds are treated in the following way:

If the compound contains one or more nouns, the principal noun takes the plural marker — *attorneys-general, editors-in-chief, brothers-in-law*. If it does not contain a noun, the plural marker goes at the end of the whole compound — *sing-alongs, fill-ins, walk-ons*. There are exceptions to these rules, as there are to many 'rules' in English — for example, it is now debatable whether one should write *attorneys-general or attorney-generals*. Spoken English changes all the time, and it takes written rules a little longer to catch up. So, we might say something which we still hesitate to put into writing. A good guide to follow when such dilemmas occur is 'Err on the conservative side until you are sure that the innovation is acceptable'.

Possession in nouns

One problem area that deserves special attention is the spelling of words that show **possession**. In English we use the apostrophe to show possession in nouns (words that name things) — so: *This is John's desk. The book's cover is torn. The children's singing was charming. It is nearly the animals' feeding time*. How can you learn where to put the apostrophe?

There is a very simple rule which you can apply to all nouns in the English language. First, realise that the apostrophe is not inserted *into* anything — it is always placed immediately *after* the possessing noun. Here is the three-step rule that you can follow:

Step 1 *Write the possessing noun down.* It may be a singular or plural noun — just write it in whichever is the appropriate form.

Step 2 *Add an apostrophe.* This is an automatic procedure — don't even think about it.

Step 3 *Decide whether an s after the apostrophe is needed.* Say the word aloud. If it sounds right without the *s*, stop at the apostrophe. If it only sounds right when you add the *s*, add it.

Examples:

the book of the boy
Step 1: boy (possessing noun)
Step 2: boy'
Step 3: boy's (add *s* because *boy'* + *book* alone sounds wrong)
the boy's book

the tiara of the duchess
Step 1: duchess
Step 2: duchess'
Step 3: duchess' OR duchess's (optional — which do you prefer when you
say it aloud?)
the duchess' tiara OR *the duchess's tiara*

the house of the Joneses (Joneses is the plural of Jones)
Step 1: Joneses
Step 2: Joneses'
Step 3: Joneses' (an extra s would sound ridiculous!)
the Joneses' house

Exercise

Complete these sentences by completing the possessive form of the noun in
italics:
1 The *boy____* coat is on the chair.
2 The *princess____* tiara is set with diamonds.
3 *Charles Dickens____* novels are classics.
4 Most of the *students____* books were destroyed in the fire (*students* is
   plural).
5 The *ladies____* rest room is being redecorated.
6 The *Attorney-General____* office is on the top floor.
7 The *women____* magazine will be on sale tomorrow.

Turn these 'of' forms into the form which places the possessing noun (in
italics) first:
8 The children of my *sisters-in-law* are playing happily together.
9 The houses of *Jack* and *Bill* are in the same street (separate ownership).
10 The mother of *Martha and Tammy* is in the garden (joint ownership).

Solutions

1 boy's; 2 princess's; 3 Dickens' OR Dickens's; 4 students'; 5 ladies'; 6 Attorney-General's;
7 women's; 8 My sisters-in-law's children; 9 Jack's and Bill's houses; 10 Martha and
Tammy's mother.

Sometimes the 'of' form is preferable. It just sounds odd to say *the table's top*
or *the car's door*. In these instances, usually concerning inanimate objects, we
write *the top of the table* and *the door of the car*. An alternative is to use the
possessing noun as an adjective and omit the idea of possession altogether — *the
table top* and *the car door*. The apostrophe is also omitted when a plural noun
is used as an adjective immediately before the noun in the title of an organisation
or institution, so *Students' Union* becomes *Students Union*. The context of what
you are writing will tell you which version to use.

Possession in *pronouns* (see page 56) is different — no apostrophe is used in
a possessive pronoun. For example: ***His** coat is on **its** hook. **Their** books are on
the table. That umbrella is **yours.*** English pronouns retain a case system from
earlier forms of English and from Latin influence, so they change depending on

how the pronoun is to be used in a sentence. The personal pronoun *I*, for instance, is *I* when it is the subject in a sentence, *me* when it is the object, *my* when it is possessive and the thing possessed is stated — *mine* when it is not stated. For example: *I am the owner of that umbrella. Please give it to me. That is my umbrella. I repeat — it is mine.*

Do not confuse possession with **contraction** (see page 57) If you remember that pronouns never contain apostrophes, you should have no difficulty when words sound the same.

Examples:
its = belonging to it (possessive)
it's = it is/ it has (contraction)
whose = belonging to who (possessive)
who's = who is/who has (contraction)

There are some other times when apostrophes are not used — for example:
(a) plurals of numerals — Four 15s make sixty.
(b) commonly curtailed words — *phone* (telephone), *plane* (aeroplane).

Exercise

Part A
Rewrite these sentences including apostrophes where necessary to show possession. Tick any that are correct:
1 I told them what both the consultants fees would be.
2 Boys clothes are generally rather less expensive than girls.
3 The novels of writers in the last few decades discuss the social issues of our time.
4 Last week I met my fathers three brothers wives who are three sisters.
5 Box the red pamphlets up in 100s and the blue ones in 50s.
6 Yours is the larger garden, but ours has better drainage.
7 The student from Ringwood Girls School found that it is difficult to take a cello on a bus.
8 The Harrises pool is a good place to cool off on a hot day.
9 My brother-in-laws childrens bicycles are in Mrs Marshs shed.

Part B
Rewrite these sentences including apostrophes where necessary either to show that something has been omitted (contraction) or to make something clear:
10 Mind your ps and qs and make sure you dot your is and cross your ts.
11 I invited the Greek ambassador to call at four oclock but he couldnt come.
12 Dont ask that man whos wearing the bowler hat; hell only say he doesnt know.
13 Lets go to Worcester on Tuesday; then well have time to see the cricket, wont we?
14 Weve just been to visit Walter Smith, but because hes been ill recently and hasnt properly recovered, they wouldnt let us see him.
15 There are four ss in Mississippi but theres only one M.

Solutions:

Part A
1 I told them what both the consultants' fees would be.
2 Boys' clothes are generally rather less expensive than girls'.
3 Correct.(The apostrophe is not used to indicate plural.)
4 Last week I met my father's three brothers' wives who are three sisters.
5 Correct.(No need for apostrophes as the figure+s combination is easy to read.)
6 Correct.(Possessive pronouns do not include apostrophes.)
7 Correct.('Cello, like 'phone,is no longer used; girls is a plural noun being used as an adjective.)
8 The Harrises' pool is a good place to cool off on a hot day.
9 My brother-in-law's children's bicycles are in Mrs Marsh's shed.

Part B
10 Mind your p's and q's and make sure you dot your i's and cross your t's.
11 I invited the Greek ambassador to call at four o'clock but he couldn't come.
12 Don't ask that man who's wearing the bowler hat; he'll only say he doesn't know.
13 Let's go to Worcester on Tuesday; then we'll have time to see the cricket, won't we?
14 We've just been to visit Walter Smith, but because he's been ill recently and hasn't properly recovered, they wouldn't let us see him.
15 There are four s's in Mississippi but there's only one M.

Spelling checks

Some words are spelling problems because they are similar in appearance to other words, though they may mean something entirely different. Use your dictionary to check on the meanings of words you are not sure of. In that way the context can later help you decide on the spelling.

Exercise

Part A
Write sentences to show that you know the difference in meaning between these pairs of words:

1 accept   2 infer   3 addition 4 dessert   5 Joneses
   except   imply   edition   desert   Jones's

6 accede 7 singeing 8 eminent 9 immigrate 10 its
   exceed   singing   imminent emigrate   it's

Suggested solutions

One sentence per pair has been used here sometimes — you can use one or two.

1 I think everyone will *accept* my invitation *except* my brother who will be overseas.
2 Did you *imply* that my work was below standard? I *inferred* that from the way you spoke.
3 In *addition* to the morning papers, he bought the latest *edition* of *The Bulletin*.
4 Ice cream is my favourite *dessert*. If you *desert* me, I will be miserable.
5 The *Joneses* own a swimming pool and it is Mr *Jones's* job to keep it clean.
6 I will *accede* to your request provided your expenses do not *exceed* £50.
7 She didn't notice that she was *singeing* her hair as she sat close to the fire, *singing* a song.
8 We are very excited because the *eminent* professor's visit to Cambridge is *imminent*.

9 Many people *immigrate* to Australia from Asia, but few *emigrate* from Australia to Asia.
10 *It's* a shame that the baby kangaroo has lost *its* mother.

Part B

Here are some more confusing pairs and groups of words. Make sure you can use all of them correctly in sentences.

1	negligible, negligent	9	personal, personnel
2	adopt, adapt	10	principle, principal
3	implicit, explicit	11	credible, credulous
4	allude, elude	12	migrate, immigrate, emigrate
5	officious, official, efficient	13	all ready, already
6	continual, continuous	14	affected, effected
7	amount, number	15	accept, except
8	fewer, less	16	lend, loan

Suggested solutions

1 I am glad the amount of work left is *negligible*. / The crash resulted from his *negligent* driving.
2 We intend to *adopt* a baby. / I can *adapt* to new conditions very quickly.
3 *Implicit* in his remarks was a slur on my captaincy. / An *explicit* diagram made the mechanism clear.
4 In my speech I will *allude* to your very fine work. / The burglar was able to *elude* the police for hours.
5 Nobody likes her overbearing, *officious* manner. / He is now the *official* scorer for the cricket club. / She is very *efficient* in her prompt and accurate handling of orders.
6 The teacher commented on the *continual* chatter of the students. / The torrential rain had been *continuous* for about eight hours, and the streets were now flooded.
7 Please give me a small *amount* of dessert. / A *number* of sweets were given to the children.
8 There are *fewer* people here now than were here earlier. / Give me *less* dessert than you gave him.
9 I resigned for *personal* reasons. / The *personnel* files hold details of all the people we employ here.
10 Her work is based on a sound design *principle*. / The college *principal* will retire next year.
11 Your story is quite *credible* — I believe it. / He is a *credulous* person — he'll believe anything.
12 People *migrate* from one country to another in search of better living conditions. / Many people *immigrate* to Australia from Europe. / My home is England and I do not intend to *emigrate* overseas.
13 We are *all ready* to go to the beach. / I have *already* completed the task you set me.
14 Her breathing was *affected* by the smog. /The doctor *effected* a cure in the boy who had been sick.
15 I *accept* your invitation to dinner. / Everyone is coming to the party *except* Joe.
16 Please *lend* me £10. / She made me a *loan* of £10.

Proofreading

We included *poor proofreading* in our list of faults that make documents difficult to read. One of the causes of poor proofreading is the inability to spot the difference between the right and wrong spellings of some quite common words. This applies particularly when we are proofreading our own work.

Precisely because these words are common, we tend to skip over them quickly, imagining that they must be correctly spelt, whereas we tend to take more care with the spelling of unusual words.

Comprehensive spelling and word usage exercise

1 Here are some commonly misspelt words. Tick the correct spelling (A or B) from each pair. Give yourself a time limit of, say, one and a half minutes to complete this question.

	A	B		A	B
1	accede	acsede	26	dulness	dullness
2	accomodation	accommodation	27	February	Febuary
3	benefited	benefitted	28	laid	layed
4	preceeding	preceding	29	reccomend	recommend
5	changable	changeable	30	beleive	believe
6	aplication	application	31	discribe	describe
7	disapoint	disappoint	32	misspell	mispell
8	skilful	skillful	33	umberella	umbrella
9	moveable	movable	34	grammar	grammer
10	drownded	drowned	35	referred	refered
11	differrence	difference	36	mishapen	misshapen
12	maintainance	maintenance	37	conscientous	conscientious
13	liaison	liason	38	revelant	relevant
14	comitted	committed	39	eminent	emminent
15	consensus	concensus	40	proceedure	procedure
16	equiped	equipped	41	occasionally	occassionally
17	humorous	humourous	42	advisor	adviser
18	superintendent	superintendant	43	purefy	purify
19	supersede	supercede	44	mischievous	mischievious
20	seperate	separate	45	unparallelled	unparalleled
21	posesses	possesses	46	noticeable	noticable
22	occurence	occurrence	47	coronary	coronory
23	transferral	transferal	48	mimicking	mimicing
24	contraltoes	contraltos	49	intermarrage	intermarriage
25	heros	heroes	50	sieze	seize

2 Ten sentences to be read aloud are on page 21 (Solutions, Question 2). Get a friend to read them to you exactly as printed if you would like to do this part of the exercise. One word in each sentence should be repeated. You should write this word down.

3 Choose the correct word from the list below to complete these sentences:
   a The repair to the ship cannot be _____ in so short a time.
   b The director objects not just to the details but to the _____ on which this report is based.
   c I believe the take- _____ time has been put forward by one hour.
   d You can get a replacement driving _____ from the motor registry.
   e The economist, John Wain, _____ that the gross national product will increase by less than 5 per cent this year.

   Words to choose from: off effected prophecies of licence
   principal prophesies prophesys principle license affected

4 Fill in the correct word in these sentences from those given for choice:
 a Car drivers should take the ____ route to Queensferry. (alternate, alternative)
 b If you drive a car, you must be a ____ driver. (licenced, licensed)
 c The tickets are ____, and are for Saturday. (complementary, complimentary)
 d He is ____ on his parents for pocket money. (dependant, dependent)
 e We have asked for her ____ on our problem, and we should take notice of it. (council, counsel)
 f She ____ a limp in order to get sick leave. (effected, affected)
 g During your tour, you will visit many of the ____ cities of Africa. (principal, principle)
 h Why have you decided to ____ Jimmy from today's activities? (accept, except)
 i Our new building will have twenty ____ . (stories, storeys)
 j You must ____ that you get to the interview in time. (insure, ensure)

Solutions

1 1A, 2B, 3A, 4B, 5B, 6B, 7B, 8A, 9B, 10B, 11B, 12B, 13A, 14B, 15A, 16B, 17A, 18A, 19A, 20B, 21B, 22B, 23A, 24B 25B, 26B, 27A, 28A, 29B, 30B, 31B, 32A, 33B, 34A, 35A, 36B, 37B, 38B, 39A, 40B, 41A, 42B, 43B, 44A, 45B, 46A, 47A, 48A, 49B, 50B

2 Get a friend to read these sentences to you as printed — the whole sentence followed by a repeat of the word to be written down.

 a We have a *maintenance* contract for electronic equipment. *maintenance*
 b We will start all over again from the *beginning*. *beginning*
 c I do not *usually* drink coffee. *usually*
 d Is this the letter you *referred* to? *referred*
 e My friend *receives* unemployment benefits. *receives*
 f On her new diet, she is *losing* about one kilogram a week. *losing*
 g The stain on the carpet is not really *noticeable* . *noticeable*
 h I was *surprised* to hear how well he spoke Japanese. *surprised*
 i Are you *certain* you posted those letters? *certain*
 j The *consensus* is that we should hold another meeting. *consensus*

3 a effected b principle c off d licence e prophesies

4 a alternative d dependent g principal j ensure
 b licensed e counsel h except
 c complimentary f affected i storeys

Hyphenation

Dividing words at line ends and joining words together to make compounds come under the general heading of **hyphenation**.

You should not ignore appropriate *division* of words at line-ends, even if your word processor automatically divides words for you. You need to understand the principles involved in line-end division. Some of the more important rules are set out below. For a deeper study, consult any good typewriting or keyboarding textbook.

The main rule is: divide a word where it sounds right — that is, between syllables. Never divide so that only one or two letters are carried over to the second line. *Strange-ly* is a bad division because the whole word can be fitted on the end of a typed line by using the margin release for only one letter.

Divide after a prefix or before a suffix, as in *pre-meditate, manage-ment*. Divide between doubled consonants, as in *knit-ting*. Divide at an existing hyphen and nowhere else in words like *well-bred, self-appointed*.

Some words should not be divided at all. Never divide a proper noun like *Australia* or its adjective *Australian*. Never divide words of one syllable regardless of length. Never divide a person's name unless it is very long: *Mr J Wong, Penelope, Billy-Joe* (each should be kept as a unit on one line); but a long name like

Professor Ebenezer J Branchwater-Fyffe

could cause problems, depending on where it occurred on the line. If necessary, such a name can be divided (without a hyphen) before the surname —

> ... to thank our highly respected guest, *Professor Ebenezer J Branchwater-Fyffe* for his interesting talk ...

Exercise

Where could you divide each of these words at line ends? Some could be divided in several places while some cannot be divided at all:

frighten, abilities, Marion, justify, linguist, overthrow, knowledgeable, omission, corroborate, well-appointed,merciful, royal, strangely, knitting, self-respect, solicitor-general, Lady Helena J Brackenridge-Leggatt, strengths, Canberra.

Solutions

frighten, royal, strangely: do not divide because any reasonable division would leave only two letters on the second line
abilities — abili-ties
Marion, Canberra: do not divide proper names
justify — jus-tify
linguist — lin-guist
knitting — knit-ting
overthrow — over-throw
knowledgeable — knowledge-able
omission — omis-sion
corroborate — cor-robo-rate
well-appointed, self-respect, solicitor-general : at existing hyphen only
merciful — merci-ful
strengths: do not divide words of one syllable, however long
Lady Helena J Brackenridge-Leggatt: Lady Helena J || Brackenridge-Leggatt

Hyphenation is also used to make a *compound* word, to distinguish between two words spelt the same but having entirely different meanings, to break up awkward combinations of letters, to mark some prefixes, and to write out some numbers and fractions. These uses are detailed in the Punctuation section (see page 52).

4 Parts of speech

Words are classified according to their function in sentences. These word classes are called parts of speech. There are eight parts of speech in English: noun, pronoun, verb, adjective, adverb, preposition, conjunction and interjection. We will look at each of them here briefly.

Usually a part of speech consists of just one word, but its function can be performed by a group of words (a phrase) or a whole clause (sentence). For example, look at these three sentences:

The *aim* is what we have to keep in mind all the time.

Preventing trouble is what we have to keep in mind all the time.

How we should prevent trouble is what we have to keep in mind all the time.

The second part of the sentence is the same in each example. The beginning of the sentence, the subject, means the same in each sentence, but the function of naming is expressed in the first by a single noun, in the second by a noun phrase and in the third by a noun clause.

The labels noun, noun phrase and noun clause are the kinds of terms you need if you are to be able to talk about writing. You need them to help you understand sentence structure and therefore paragraph structure and document structure; and you need them to help you explain to others how their writing could be improved by making sure that these parts of speech are used correctly.

Noun

Nouns name things. There are several **types** of noun — common, proper, collective and abstract.

Common nouns name everyday things that you can touch:

> The *children* used the *table* as a *Wendy house* and held a *party* with their *dolls*.

Proper nouns name particular things and always begin with a capital letter:

> *Joe* visited *Carlisle* on *Sunday* and stayed at the *Royal Hotel*.

Collective nouns name groups of things:

> The huge *audience* was cheering as the winning basketball *team* col-

lected their medals. (Note that singular collective nouns can have singular or plural connotations, depending on whether they are regarded as single units or separate individuals in a given context. For example: (1) the jury *was considering its* verdict (singular, because the jury here is acting as one unit); (2) the jury dispersed to *their* respective homes after the trial (plural, because here the jury means 'the individual members of the jury').

Abstract nouns name things that you cannot touch, like feelings and emotions:

'*Happiness* is the *freedom* to do what you want' he said.

Nouns also have number, gender and case.

Number indicates whether there is one or more than one of the given noun. Plural number is marked by one of the regular or irregular plural markers (see page 14).

Gender is sometimes marked by a special ending, for example *-or/-ess*, as in *actor* (masculine) and *actress* (feminine). However, gender marking is disappearing rapidly from writing, so that it is becoming more usual to use *actor* for both male and female stage performers. Most nouns are neuter.

Case of English nouns is nowadays only clear from the position and function of the noun in the sentence: this is because the noun does not change whether it is the subject or the object. Only the possessive case alters the noun. The following examples may make the point clearer:

The *typist* (subjective case) made six copies of the report.

The manager praised the *typist* (objective case) on the quality of the reports.

The *typist's* (possessive case) work was excellent.

Exercise

Identify the nouns in these sentences and say as much as you can about their type, number, gender and case:

The congregation in the church on Sunday prayed for peace.
One boy in the choir gave the other boys a fright by dropping all the books.
The news was given to Peter's parents by the constable.

Solutions

congregation (collective, singular, neuter, subjective)
church (common, sing., neuter, obj.)
Sunday (proper, sing., neuter, obj.)
peace (abstract, sing., neuter, obj.)
boy (common, sing., masculine, subj.)
choir (collective, sing., neuter, obj.)
boys (common, plural, masc., indirect obj.)
fright (abstract, sing., neuter, obj.)
books (common, pl, neuter, obj.)
news (common, sing., neuter, subj.)
Peter's (proper, sing., masc., possessive)
parents (common, pl, common, obj.)
constable (common, sing., common, obj.)

You will have noticed that nouns can be, and often are, preceded by *a*, *an* or *the*. These little words are called **articles** (or sometimes 'determiners'). Articles are sometimes discussed as separate parts of speech and sometimes included among adjectives. As they only ever occur with nouns and noun phrases, or with words functioning as nouns, a short comment here is all that is necessary.

A and *an* are called **indefinite articles**. While *a* is used before a noun or noun phrase beginning with a consonant (*a* book, *a* ripe apple), *an* is used before a noun or noun phrase beginning with a vowel (*an* apple, *an* exciting story). Some people use *an* before words starting with the letter *h* (eg *an hotel*), but this is not modern English — it is pronunciation of words that English has borrowed from French, in the way French people would say them.

The is the definite article and is used before any noun or noun phrase when we want to specify a particular thing or things: This is *the book* I want. One of *the most hilarious stories* went like this.

Pronoun

Pronouns stand instead of nouns. If we had no pronouns, we would have to write sentences like:

> When Pat arrived at Pat's office, Pat made Pat a cup of coffee and read the paper the secretary had given Pat.

As we have pronouns, we can leave most of the repetition of *Pat* out and write:

> When *Pat* arrived at *his* office, *he* made *himself* a cup off coffee and read the paper the secretary had given *him*.

He, him and *his* are different cases of the same personal pronoun — some pronouns change their form depending on their grammatical function. *He* is subjective, *him* is objective and *his* is possessive.

Himself is a **reflexive** pronoun — this group, always ending in *-self* or *-selves*, is only used when the subject acts upon itself (*he hurt himself*) or to emphasise that the subject acted alone (*she did it herself*).

There are several types of pronoun:

personal: I, you, we, they, him, them, his, my, our, ours etc
I gave *you my* books and *they* gave *him yours*.

reflexive: myself, itself, yourself, yourselves, themselves etc
He warmed *himself* by the fire.

relative: who, whom, whose, which, that, what
The person *whose* book I found is the same person *who* lent me the paper *that* is missing.

interrogative: who, whom, whose, which, what
Whose book is missing? *Who* had it last? *What* was it about?

demonstrative: this, that, these, those
This is mine, but *that* belongs with *those*.

indefinite: any, each, several, some, etc
Have you *any*? There are *several* in the kitchen.

Like nouns, some pronouns have number and case. The case system of pronouns is one of the last relics in English of a Latin case system.

Person is another such relic. It is a means of classifying personal pronouns as follows: first person is the person speaking (*I, me, we, us*), second person is the person spoken to (*you*) and third person is the person spoken about (*he, him, she, her, it, they, them*). For instance:

> I am speaking to you about them. (*I* is first person, *you* is second person, *them* is third person)

> We are going to the theatre with him and her. (*We* is first person, *him* and *her* are third person — notice that they are also in the objective case ; this is because they follow the preposition *with*)

Gender is also shown (*she, he, him, her* etc), but modern English does not have a neutral pronoun to use in sentences like these:

> When the applicant completes the form, *he/she* should lodge it at the post office.

> Somebody left *her/his* pen here last night.

There is a growing tendency to use *they* and *their* in a singular sense to cover these situations:

> Somebody left *their* pen here last night when *they* finished work.

Contrary to some people's beliefs, singular *they* is not new — it is a return to an old form which was in common usage until grammarians decreed that *they* could only be used in the plural. It is more logical and workable to accept singular *they* than to impose a new pronoun. This topic is discussed further on page 73.

Other solutions are to make the whole sentence plural, or to use the passive voice of the verb:

> When applicants complete forms, they should lodge them at the post office.

> When the form is completed, it should be lodged at the post office.

A 'plain English' solution is to use the pronoun *you* when direct address is involved:

> When *you* complete the form, *you* should lodge it at the post office.

Exercise

Spot all the pronouns in these sentences. Try to describe them as fully as possible by giving their type, number, gender (if applicable) and case.

1 She went to find them and they had tangled themselves in the wool.
2 Several had gone to see those, but most stayed here with these.
3 Who gave you that?
4 There is the man whom she is going to marry.
5 Who did this?
6 It's her book.

Solutions

1 she (personal, fem, singular, subjective); them (personal, plural, objective).
  they (personal, pl, subj.); themselves (reflexive, pl, obj.).
2 several (indefinite, pl, subj.); those (demonstrative, pl, obj.); most (indef, pl, subj.); these
  (demonstrative, pl, obj.)
3 who (interrogative, sing./pl, subj.); you (personal, sing./pl, obj.); that (demons, sing, obj.)
4 whom (personal, sing., masculine by inference, obj.); she (personal, fem, sing, subj.)
5 who (interrog, sing., subj); this (demonstrative, sing., obj.)
6 it (personal, neuter, sing, subj.); her (personal, fem., sing., possessive).

Verb

The verb is the most important word or group of words in the sentence. In fact, a sentence can consist of a verb on its own:

> Stop!

There are many ways to classify verbs and the ways they work. Here are some of the most important:

• Verbs can be either doing (or action) words, or linking words.

> The dog *chased* the postman. (*chased* tells what action was going on)

> The postman *is* a middle-aged man. (*is* links *postman* and *middle-aged man* — they are one and the same; this type of sentence is known as 'equational')

• Verbs are transitive or intransitive. **Transitive** means that action passes across from the subject of the sentence to an object. **Intransitive** means that there is no action passing across.

> The student *read* her book. (*read* is transitive — action is passing across from *student* to *her book*)

> That child *grizzles* all the time. (*grizzles* is intransitive — no action is passing across from *that child* to anything)

• Verbs are active or passive. **Active voice** means that the agent (doer of an action) is in subject position of the sentence, with the recipient of the action in object position. **Passive voice** means that the recipient of the action is in subject position, while the agent (if any) is in object position.

> The committee *has rejected* your application for membership. (*has rejected* is active)

> Your application for membership *has been rejected* by the committee. (*has been rejected* is passive — the agent is in object position)

> Your application for membership *has been rejected*. (*has been rejected* is passive — in this construction the agent has been omitted)

• Verbs have **tense** — that is, they express time. The three main tenses are simple past, present and future, as in

> Yesterday I *spoke* to my grandmother. (past)

> Today I *speak* to you. (present)

> Tomorrow I *shall speak* to another group. (future)

• Verbs can consist of one or several words; when more than one word is used, the verb is a *verb phrase*. Verb phrases consist of the main verb plus one or more auxiliaries which help to show tense (past, present, future), voice (whether it is active or passive) and aspect (whether it is still going on or has been completed).

> Jo *works* hard. (*works* is a one-word verb — the following examples use forms of the main verb *work* plus auxiliaries)
>
> Jo *has worke*d for several employers.
>
> Jo *is working* on your report.
>
> Jo *has been working* for more than an hour.
>
> Jo *will have been working* for two hours soon.

• Verbs have parts called participles which are used with auxiliaries (often part of the verbs *be* or *have*) to form more complex tenses etc. In the examples above, *work* is the basic verb, *working* is its present participle and *worked* is its past participle. Most verbs follow this *-ing*, *-ed* (or *-t*) pattern, but there are many exceptions. Consult a dictionary if you are not sure of the correct spelling of a participle. Here are only a few examples, beginning with two regular formations and continuing with some that cause problems because their past tenses and past participles are irregular:

Verb	Present	Present Ptcple.	Past	Past Ptcple.
to dream	dream	dreaming	dreamt	dreamt
to walk	walk	walking	walked	walked
to run	run	running	ran	run
to bear	bear	bearing	bore	borne
to go	go	going	went	gone
to rise	rise	rising	rose	risen

Some groups of verbs cause special difficulty. One group is *lay/lie*:

Verb	Present	Present Ptcple.	Past	Past Ptcple.
to lay(to put down)	lay	laying	laid	laid
to lie (to recline)	lie	lying	lay	lain
to lie (to tell untruths)	lie	lying	lied	lied

Here are sentences containing all these forms:

> I always *lay* the table for dinner.
>
> The hens are *laying* well at the moment.
>
> He *laid* the books on the desk.
>
> The rumour was *laid* to rest by the principal.
>
> I *lie* on my couch when I need a nap.
>
> She is *lying* on the floor.
>
> He *lay* in the sun for too long today.
>
> The patient has *lain* on his back for an hour now.
>
> Some people *lie* about their ages.
>
> She was *lying* when she said she hated music.
>
> The witness was charged with perjury because he *lied* on oath.
>
> He has *lied* all his life — he is unlikely to start telling the truth now.

Keep the parts of verb phrases together as far as possible. It is difficult to read a passage in which the verbs are consistently split. It is thus better to write:

> The student *was glancing* at the clock surreptitiously and rather anxiously every few minutes.

than to write:

> The student *was* surreptitiously and rather anxiously *glancing* at the clock every few minutes.

Verbs must agree with their subjects in person (first, second, third) and number (singular or plural).

> I *am* a teacher. (*am* is first person singular to agree with *I* which is the same)

> He *is* a student. (*is* is third person singular to agree with *he* which is the same)

> A box of books *was* delivered today. (*was* is singular to agree with *a box* which is also singular and is the real subject of the sentence)

> The news *is* bad today. (*is* is singular to agree with *news* which is a singular noun despite its final *s*)

> Toast and marmalade *is* my favourite breakfast. (*is* is singular to agree with the singular compound *toast and marmalade*)

Exercise

1 Underline the verbs and say whether they are *action* or *linking* verbs:
Frank Jones is the Managing Director of the company.
He directs the work of hundreds of people.
I have read your report, and I think it is excellent.
She is leaving next week and her position has been advertised in the paper.
2 Underline the verbs and say whether they are *transitive* or *intransitive*:
The supervisor has read your report and thanks you for your promptness.
The old lady smiled as her daughter opened the car door for her.
When the student was praised for her presentation, she blushed profusely.
He melted the butter in the pan while I almost melted in the hot sun.
3 Underline the verbs and say whether they are *active* or *passive*:
The director has approved your application but mine has been rejected.
Dogs must be kept on a lead when they are walked on farmland.
Keep your dog on a lead when you walk it on farmland.
4 Underline the verbs and say what *tense* each one is:
The baritone sang an aria from the opera he will perform in Milan.
Her writing improves all the time because she uses a dictionary for spelling problems.
This report was written by James who is now head of the section.
5 Fill in the blanks with the correct past participles of the verbs in brackets:
a Channel 2 has (broadcast)_____ the news at 7 pm for years.
b Shane Gould had (swim) _____ for Australia before she retired.

    c I have (lay) _____ the book on the table for you.
    d If I have (lie) _____ to you, it was only to protect you from the truth.
    d She has (lie) _____ in bed for long enough; tell her to get up.
    e We will set off on our picnic as soon as the sun has (rise) _____ .
    f I think you should have (rid) _____ yourself of that mangy animal long
      ago.
    g Have you (ride) _____ your horse lately?
6 Correct any errors of *agreement* :
    a Neither of the trees will shed their leaves until the autumn.
    b The company moved into their new office last week.
    c Bacon and eggs are still an appealing breakfast to many people.
    d Keyboarders should proofread everything they do.
    e Each of the tomatoes in the crates on the shelves have black spots.

Solutions

> 1 is (linking); directs (action); have read (action), think (action), is (linking); is leaving (action), has been advertised (action).
> 2 has read (transitive), thanks (transitive); smiled (intransitive), opened (transitive); was praised (intransitive), blushed (intransitive); melted (1) (transitive), melted (2) (intransitive).
> 3 has approved (active), has been rejected (passive); must be kept (passive), are walked (passive); keep (active), walk (active).
> 4 sang (past), will perform (future); improves (present), uses (present); was written (past), is (present).
> 5 a broadcast; b swum; c laid; d lied; e lain; f risen; g rid; h ridden
> 6 a their —> its; b their —> its; c are —> is; d correct; e have —> has

Adjective

Adjectives tell more about (modify) a noun. They are usually placed immediately before the noun, but can be in another part of the sentence:

> This is a *red* rose. (*red* modifies the noun *rose* ; both say something about the subject *this)*

> This rose is *red.* (*rose* is now the subject of the sentence, but the adjective *red* still modifies it)

Adjectives have three degrees — **positive** (when nothing is being compared), **comparative** (when two things are being compared) and **superlative** (when three or more things are being compared). The usual comparative and superlative endings are *-er* and *-est* respectively, but many long adjectives take the words *more* and *most* respectively in front of the positive form.

> Maria is a *quick* typist. (positive — no comparison involved)

> Anna is *quicker* than Maria, but Jack is the *quickest* of all. (*quicker* is comparative — Anna and Maria are the two being compared; *quickest* is superlative — Jack is being compared with both Anna and Maria)

> 'Peace' is a *beautiful* rose. (positive)

> 'Peace' is *more beautiful* than 'Princess Grace'. (comparative)

> 'Woburn Abbey' is the *most beautiful* rose in the garden. (superlative)

Some adjectives are irregular in their comparative and superlative formations. Here are a few:

good	better	best
far	further	furthest
ill	worse	worst
much	more	most
little	less	least

Some adjectives do not have degrees of comparison — nothing can be more empty than *empty*, nor could any painting or vase be more unique than *unique*.

Adjectives include words which act like them, although they are primarily different parts of speech — nouns, as in *cattle* truck, *parcel* post etc, and participles of verbs, as in *rising* sun, *working* man, *fallen* idol, *broken* dream etc. None of these forms have degrees of comparison either.

Words can be joined together with hyphens to form compound adjectives:

A *ten-year-old* girl won first prize in the mathematics competition.

The hyphens are not needed when the words do not immediately precede the noun they modify:

First prize was won by a girl who was *ten years old*.

Exercise
Correct the misused adjectives in these sentences:
1 Of methods A and B, A is the more simpler way to follow
2 The soprano sings good, but the most great singer I ever heard was a tenor.

Solutions

1 more simpler —> simpler; 2 good —> well, most great —> greatest

Adverb
Adverbs tell more about (modify) a verb, an adjective or another adverb. They can usually be identified easily because of their *-ly* ending, but not always: for instance, *cowardly* is an adjective and *fast* can be an adjective or an adverb.

Adverbs also have degrees of comparison, like adjectives, and their comparative and superlative formations are arrived at in much the same way as those of adjectives. The most common formation is to place *more* and *most* before the positive form of the adverb. Here are a few examples:

quickly	more quickly	most quickly
beautifully	more beautifully	most beautifully

Some adverbs have the same form as adjectives. For example:

This is a *hard* examination. (adjective) The team worked *hard*. (adverb)

Tony owns a *fast* boat. (adjective) The ship was stuck *fast* on the mud. (adverb)

Such adverbs form their comparative and superlative degrees in the same way as the adjectives:

| hard | harder | hardest |
| fast | faster | fastest |

There are irregularly formed adverbs too, for example:

| well | better | best |
| badly | worse | worst |

Here are some sentences which show adverbs being used correctly in various situations:

Maria types *quickly*, but Anna types *more quickly* than Maria and Jack types *most quickly* of all. (adverbs in various degrees modifying the verb *types*)

This is a *very* fast train. (*very* modifies the adjective *fast*)

The early train travels *quite* slowly. (*quite* modifies the adverb *slowly*)

Her flight arrived *early*. (*early* here is an adverb modifying the verb *arrived*; in the previous sentence *early* is an adjective modifying the noun *train*)

There are some words which usually function as adverbs but can also be adjectives, and which should be placed in sentences carefully because they affect the meaning of the whole sentence. One of these is *only*. Try placing it in various places in a sentence and see how the meaning changes:

1 *Only* Tammy bought cakes at the supermarket yesterday. (she was the only person)

2 Tammy *only* bought cakes at the supermarket yesterday. (she didn't sell any herself)

3 Tammy bought *only* cakes at the supermarket yesterday. (she didn't buy biscuits as well)

4 Tammy bought cakes *only* at the supermarket yesterday. (she didn't go to another shop)

5 Tammy bought cakes at the *only* supermarket yesterday. (there is only one supermarket)

6 Tammy bought cakes at the supermarket *only* yesterday. (the cakes are still fresh)

7 Tammy bought cakes at the supermarket yesterday *only*. (she didn't shop on any other day)

Exercise

Insert the appropriate comparative or superlative form of the adverb in brackets:
1 John speaks (quickly) _____ than his brother.
2 Of them all, she spoke (distinctly)_____ .
3 During the gale, our boat rode out the storm (well) _____ of all.
4 Franco works (hard) _____ than most people in the shop.
5 Tim behaves (badly) _____ than his sister.

Solutions

Preposition

Prepositions are often confused with adverbs. They frequently have the same form, but their functions are very different. Whereas an adverb modifies a verb, for example, and has no relation to any other word in the sentence, as in

The child had to stay *in* as punishment. (*in* modifies the verb *stay*)

The spider climbed *up* while I watched. (*up* modifies the verb *climbed*)

a preposition shows the relationship between two things. It shows where one thing is in relation to another. A preposition is always followed by a noun or pronoun (or their equivalents), and the pronoun is always in the objective case:

The child had to stay *in* the classroom as punishment. (*in* is a preposition showing the relation between *child* and *classroom* — *in the classroom* is a prepositional phrase)

The spider climbed *up* the tree trunk while I watched. (*up* is a preposition showing the relation between *spider* and *tree trunk* — *up the tree trunk* is a prepositional phrase)

We walked *across* the road, *into* the garden, *past* the dustbins, *into* the house and *up* the stairs. (*across the road* etc are prepositional phrases)

Jan is coming *with David and me*. (preposition is followed by pronoun in objective case; if you are not sure whether to use *David and I* or *David and me*, leave David out and see if what's left makes sense: *with ... I* or *with ... me*?)

There are some words which are always followed by particular prepositions. Here are just a few of them — use your dictionary to check that you are using the correct combination:

adjacent *to*	afflicted *with*	culminate *in*
dependent on	different *from*	independent *of*
opposite *to*	profit *by*	substitute *for*

and there are many others. We will discuss prepositional idioms again on page 105.

Some words can be followed by more than one preposition, depending on the meaning, as:

He fell *in* the pool. (he was already in the pool and he lost his footing)

He fell *into* the pool. (means he was standing on the edge and tipped over into the water)

I am responsible *to* my boss *for* preparing the annual report. (responsible *to* a person and *for* a task)

As we have now dealt with nouns, verbs, adjectives, adverbs and prepositions, you should be able to recognise the functions of each of them. However, there are still some traps to be wary of. There are some words which can be used in any of those functions, and you need to be careful that you are using the right word in the right place. Such a multi-function word is *down*:

I have a pillow filled with real goose *down*. (noun)

A thug would *down* me with one blow. (verb)

The *down* train is delayed because of a derailment. (adjective)

The motorist knocked the pedestrian *down*. (adverb)

He walked quickly *down* the gentle slope. (preposition)

Exercise

1   Insert appropriate *prepositions* in the blanks provided:
   a I am responsible _____ my employer _____ doing the accounts.
   b The children ran _____ the gym and waited _____ line for their teacher.
   c I put my trust _____ him; you may rely _____ him to be discreet.
   d His house, which is adjacent _____ the river, is different _____ mine.
   e David has an aptitude _____ mathematics and should benefit _____ the course.
   f Ms Jones is capable _____ good work and is eligible _____ the position.
2   Find the *prepositions* and the *prepositional phrases* in the next sentences:
   a He came from Switzerland, through France, over to England, and stayed among us a year.
   b My house, which is adjacent to the library, is different from all the other houses in the street.

Solutions

1 a to for; b into, in; c in, upon; d to, from; e for, from;f of, for.
2 a *from* Switzerland, *through* France, *over to* England, *among* us;
   b *to* the library, *from* all the other houses, *in* the street

Conjunction

Conjunctions join words, phrases and clauses, to show either similarity or contrast between them, or to create a sequence. When they join things of equal importance, they are called *co-ordinating* conjunctions. *And* joins like things, *but* joins unlike things, and *or* joins contrasting things:

Pete *and* Mary agreed to play tennis *or* golf.

They both prefer tennis, *but* it started to rain.

When conjunctions join subordinate clauses (which cannot stand by themselves) to main clauses, they are called *subordinating* conjunctions:

We agreed *that* we would help Greg.

Greg was delayed *because* his car broke down.

When the report is finished, please put it on my desk.

Be careful not to confuse adverbs, prepositions and conjunctions. Adverbs modify, prepositions show relationships, but conjunctions merely join. You will find that the same word can function in all three ways:

We have not met *before*. (an adverb, modifying *have met*)

He stood *before* the court to plead his innocence. (a preposition — its object is *court*)

They will have lunch *before* they start work. (a subordinating conjunction joining the subordinate clause *before they start work* to the main clause *they will have lunch*)

Some conjunctions come in pairs — *both/and; not only/but also; whether/or; either/or; neither/nor*. Because they relate to two objects, they are sometimes called co-relative conjunctions. When you use these pairs, make sure that the conjunctions both come before the words they join:

(Incorrect)

My sister *neither **was*** at work *nor* at home. (This is wrong because *neither* has been placed before the verb was, whereas *nor* is not followed by a verb.)

(Correct)

My sister was *neither **at work*** nor ***at home***.

Some words are included here which may also be called transitions because they lead from one idea to another; they include *however, moreover, nevertheless*.

I am very tired; *however*, I will go to the charity ball with you.

She was the best student in college this year. *Moreover*, she topped the state in maths.

There is a lot of work still to do; *nevertheless*, it has to be done tonight.

Exercise

Fill in the blanks with appropriate *conjunctions*:

1 Henry slept in this morning ____ he was on vacation.
2 He would have liked to take a hot shower ____ the water was cold.
3 Jennifer was not sure ____ to wear a dress ____ jeans.
4 ____ Henry finally got up, he ate a large serving of eggs ____ bacon; ____, he declined toast and marmalade.
5 The Ffyffe-Robertsons own ____ a Rolls Royce ____ a Mercedes.
6 Alison is ____ fat ____ thin; she is average size for her age.
7 Her handwriting is good ____ her spelling is accurate.
8 She is conscientious ____ lacks method.
9 You can have the ice cream ____ the fruit but not both.
10 ____ it rained, we could not go to the beach, ____ we still had our picnic ____ the beach umbrella looked strange in the living room.

Solutions

(there may be alternatives):

> 1 because; 2 but; 3 whether/or; 4 when, and, however; 5 both/and; 6 neither/nor; 7 and; 8 but; 9 or;10 because, but, although

Interjection

An interjection is a word uttered in surprise, shock, great joy etc. It cannot be analysed except to identify it as an interjection:

Oh! I didn't know you were coming.

His illness, *alas*, prevents his attendance.

As interjections are rarely used in business writing, we will not consider them any further.

Here is a comprehensive exercise based on most of the parts of speech we have been discussing:

Exercise

1 Put one suitable *noun* in each of the blanks:
   I bought a _____ at the _____ yesterday _____ .
   The clapping of the _____ at the concert was deafening; they were show
   ing their _____ .
   She has two _____ which she keeps in a cage.
2 Put one suitable *pronoun* in each of the blanks:
   Jan took _____ coat off when _____ arrived in the office. Then _____ made
   _____ a cup of coffee before settling down to do _____ work.
3 Put one suitable *verb* or *verb part* in each of the blanks (you may have to
   use more than one word):
   The doctor _____ the sick child. The child had been _____ by another
   doctor but _____ not getting any better. He _____ stung by a wasp.
4 Put one suitable *adjective* in each of the blanks:
   My hair is bright _____ in colour, but my friend's hair is _____ .
   Fortunately, this report is much _____ than the last one, but Jo's is the
   _____ of all.
5 Put one suitable *adverb* in each of the blanks:
   She works _____ so she can leave _____ today.
   I slammed on the brakes and stopped the car _____ .
6 Put one suitable *preposition* in each of the blanks:
   I was swimming _____ the pool when I saw a child fall _____ it.
   My house is adjacent _____ the school.
   He is responsible _____ the accountant _____ getting the balance right.
7 Put one suitable *conjunction* in each of the blanks:
   We are moving to Bristol to live, _____ we are looking forward to the move
   very much.
   Our friends are moving to London, _____ they are not looking forward to the
   move.
   Jake got up later than usual _____ he was on holiday.
   _____ he got up, he ate a plateful of scrambled eggs _____ bacon _____
   drinking three cups of coffee!

Suggested solutions

1 magazine, bookshop, afternoon (common nouns) ; audience (collective n) , appreciation (abstract n) ; budgerigars (plural n)
2 her, she, she, herself, her
3 attended, treated, was, had been
4 copper, black; shorter (comparative) , shortest (superlative)
5 quickly, early; suddenly
6 in, into; to; to, for
7 and; but (both co-ordinating conjunctions) ; because (subordinate conj) ; after, and, while

Now you can identify the parts of speech in English. Of what practical use is this?

First, knowledge about words and their functions makes you more confident in using them correctly. You no longer have to rely on intuition. You know that certain words can be used in certain circumstances, and that others cannot. You know that most parts of speech have different forms (such as plurals of nouns, cases of pronouns, tenses of verbs), and you are able to use the appropriate form for any given occasion. In short, you are in control — never again do you need to feel that writing correct English is a matter of sheer luck.

Second, you will now start to develop the ability to recognise errors in construction as you begin to make them. For example, you might start to write 'The typists work quick and quiet...' but your new knowledge will stop you from completing it because you will recognise that 'quick' and 'quiet' are adjectives which can only modify nouns — what you need here are adverbs to modify the verb 'work'. So you switch to writing the -*ly* adverbs 'quickly' and 'quietly'. You will hesitate a lot initially, but after a while, it will become more automatic to use the correct forms of words as you compose.

Third, you will start to see these different forms of the parts of speech and their correct (or incorrect) usage in material that others write. You will feel an affinity with the writing — no longer will it be so many black marks on paper. If you supervise the writing of others, you will be able to explain how that writing could be improved by pointing out the errors that the writer has made in the form or function of the words used.

Now that you know more about words, let us proceed to the next part of the book, which deals with putting the words together into larger chunks.

5 Groups of words: phrases, clauses, sentences

People do not think in single words as a rule. Expressions like the following are unusual, and generally restricted to emotional comments or other very special situations:

Damn!

Beautiful!

Yes?

Even these surface single word expressions have whole sentences as their underlying meaning:

Damn! (I've locked my keys in the car.)

Beautiful! (I wish I could play a backhand like that.)

Yes? (Hurry up and say what you want so that I can get back to my crossword.)

Mostly we think in groups of words, and we certainly need to write in groups of words that will be understandable to our readers. Just as you learned that there are some rules for the use of parts of speech so that they will be clear to the reader, so there are rules for the formation of groups of words. Look at this group of words:

Reference your report of 15 June on fire precautions.

Something probably tells you that there is something wrong with it, but you may not be able to say exactly what the matter is. Look at this:

I refer to your report of 15 June on fire precautions.

That is much better, isn't it? It seems to be complete. Why? Because it now has a subject and a complete verb.

This kind of rule is not something that you can tell by intuition. When you see a phrase you may say 'it seems wrong' or 'it doesn't make sense', but intuition is no substitute for knowing that an error of grammar or syntax has been made and being able to put it right. Knowing how to do that comes from knowing how acceptable English sentences are put together.

Sentence

A sentence is a group of words that is a complete thought on its own. Its meaning is complete, and nothing needs to be added to it to make it seem right instead of wrong. It does not get this way without some organisation. How is a sentence organised?

Every sentence must have a **subject**, (see discussion of case on page 24) and a **predicate**. The subject is what the sentence is about while the predicate is what is said about the subject. The subject is always a noun, pronoun or group of words that functions in the same way as a noun. The predicate must contain a complete, finite verb, but it can also contain any amount of extra information which gives more meaning to the verb.

Subject	Predicate
My husband	*arrived.*
I	*met* him at the station.
To swim in the river	*is* fun.
You	*have* five minutes left before tea time.

These sentences have only one subject and one finite verb—they are therefore called **simple sentences**. A sentence is simple also when it has either a compound subject or a compound predicate, since these represent basically only one idea each:

Subject	Predicate
My son and *my daughter*	arrived with my husband.
The savage dog	*bit* and *scratched* the child.

A **compound sentence** is one in which two or more simple sentences (or main clauses) are added together:

Jim likes playing football | | and Paul likes playing tennis | | but Mark prefers to watch it all on TV.

A **complex sentence** is one in which one or more subordinate clauses are added to at least one main clause:

We went to the beach | | because it was a fine day.

Here we have to introduce a few more terms to explain some of the paragraphs above. Let's stick to just brief definitions of phrase and clause and give examples of the most common types of each.

Phrase

A phrase is a group of words that hangs together in that it has some sense of its own, but it cannot stand alone as it is not a complete idea.
• The most easily recognisable type of phrase is the *prepositional phrase* beginning with a preposition which is always followed by a noun or pronoun in the objective case (under the chair, in the book, through the gate, with

David and me, for him).

- Other types of phrases include *verb phrases* (can apply, would have been done) and *noun phrases* (the man, the tall man, the tall thin well-dressed salesperson).

Clause

A clause is a part of a sentence that contains both a subject and a complete verb. Clauses are joined in sentences by conjunctions or by punctuation that does the same job as a conjunction. Strictly, a clause can be a simple sentence (Ms O'Sullivan is the new manager of the business). However, for our purposes, it is easier to think of a clause as *part* of the sentence. Here are some examples showing different ways of joining clauses:

Ms O'Sullivan is the new manager of the business *and* she is doing a great job. (two main clauses joined by the co-ordinating conjunction *and*)

Ms O'Sullivan is the new manager of the business; she is doing a great job. (two main clauses joined by the semi-colon)

Ms O'Sullivan, *who* is the new manager of the business, has redecorated the showroom *because* it was very shabby. (one main clause with a subordinate *who* clause embedded in it and another subordinate *because* clause added)

Some people play tennis, some people play golf, some people play netball *but* some people play no sport at all. (four main clauses: the first three joined by commas and the fourth joined by the co-ordinating conjunction *but*)

- A **main clause** can stand alone. It is sometimes called an independent clause. You can make a compound sentence by joining two or more main clauses together by using co-ordinating conjunctions. The most commonly used conjunctions for this purpose are *and*, *but*, and *or*.

- A **subordinate clause** cannot stand alone. It is sometimes called a dependent clause, because it needs a main clause to hang onto. When you join a subordinate clause to a main clause, you use a subordinating conjunction to introduce the subordinate clause. This forms a complex sentence (that is a mixture of main and subordinate), and you can add more of both types of clause, so long as your sentence does not become unwieldy. There are many subordinating conjunctions including *because, who, which, as, when, if, although, where.*

Exercise

Part A

Identify these groups of words as *phrases, main clauses,* or *subordinate clauses*:

1 under the chair

2 let's rake up the leaves
3 without a care in the world
4 he worked with a will
5 the black dog
6 the report is very comprehensive
7 that you have written
8 when you have finished this exercise
9 Spot bit the postman
10 the ball rolled out of sight
11 his sister helped him
12 before it rains

Part B
Now try to put them together in various ways to make different kinds of sentences.

Part C
Here are some sentences. Identify them as *simple, compound* or *complex*:
1 The dog barked at the messenger.
2 The dog barked at the messenger and the files fell to the floor.
3 The dog barked at the messenger who was delivering the files to my office.
4 The dog and the cat played in the yard.
5 The dog barked and snarled at the messenger.
6 I like to swim, you like to play tennis, but my mother doesn't play any sport at all.
7 The lamb followed Mary wherever she went.

Solutions

Part A

1	under the chair	prepositional phrase
2	let's rake up the leaves	main clause
3	without a care in the world	two prepositional phrases
4	he worked with a will	main clause
5	the black dog	noun phrase
6	the report is very comprehensive	main clause
7	that you have written	subordinate clause
8	when you have finished this exercise	subordinate clause
9	Spot bit the postman	main clause
10	the ball rolled out of sight	main clause
11	his sister helped him	main clause
12	before it rains	subordinate clause

Part B
Suggested solutions (there are many others):
1 The ball rolled out of sight under the chair.
2 Spot, the black dog, bit the postman.
3 The report that you have written is very comprehensive.
4 When you have finished this exercise, let's rake up the leaves before it rains.
5 He worked with a will, without a care in the world, and his sister helped him.

Part C
1 simple; 2 compound; 3 complex; 4 simple; 5 simple; 6 compound; 7 complex

Sentence functions

Sentences can be classified according to their functions. Here are the main sentence functions with an example of each:

- *Statement*: The children teased the cat.
- *Question*: Did the children tease the cat?
- *Command*: Stop teasing the cat!
- *Exclamation*: What a beautiful cat that is!

Each of these sentences has a subject and a predicate as usual, but sometimes it is difficult to see the formal structure in sentences other than straightforward statements:

	Subject	**Predicate**
Statement:	The children	<u>teased</u> the cat.
Question:	The children	<u>did...tease</u> the cat?
Command:	(You)*	<u>stop</u> teasing the cat!
Exclamation:	That	<u>is</u> what a beautiful cat!

* A command sentence often does not include an obvious subject — in this case the subject is whoever is being spoken to — *you*; it is in brackets here to indicate that it is 'understood'. The same (imperative) mood of the verb is used for polite requests too.

Exercise

Part A

Say whether these sentences are *statement, question, command, exclamation*. Try to identify the *subject* and *predicate* of each, and underline the *whole verb* in each.

1 Will John and Mary be coming to the meeting with us?
2 Ann and Peter will be coming to the meeting.
3 Please file these papers, Jane.
4 Stop talking!
5 What a pretty hat you are wearing!

Solutions

		Subject	**Predicate**
1	Question	John and Mary	*will... be coming* to the meeting with us?
2	Statement	Ann and Peter	*will be coming* to the meeting.
3	Command (request)	Jane	please *file* these papers.
4	Command	(You)	*stop* talking!
5	Exclamation	You	*are wearing* what a pretty hat!

Exercise

Part B

1 Make complete *simple* sentences by filling in the blanks appropriately:
   (a) _____ is a very kind person.

(b) The person at the next desk _____ .

2 Make complete *compound* sentences by filling in the blanks appropriately:
   (a) She finished her report very quickly _____ she still had more work to do.
   (b) I must do this work straight away _____ my supervisor will be angry.

3 Make complete *complex* sentences by filling in the blanks appropriately:
   (a) We went to the beach on Saturday _____ .
   (b) _____ , we all went home.

4 Write a *simple* sentence containing a *compound subject*.

5 Write a *compound* sentence containing *three main clauses*.

6 Write a *complex* sentence containing *one main clause, one subordinate adjective clause* and *one subordinate adverb clause*.

Suggested solutions

1 (a) My boss (subject)
   (b) has been helping me all afternoon (predicate)
2 (a) but
   (b) or (both co-ordinating conjunctions)
3 (a) because it was a sunny day (subordinate clause)
   (b) When it started to rain (subordinate clause — followed by a comma when placed first in the sentence)
4 *The director, the assistant director and the secretary* travelled together to the show.
5 *I like ice cream, you like pancakes* and *Jeri likes rice pudding.*
6 *My boss likes me to write clearly* (main clause) *because our documents are written for the general public* (subordinate adverb clause of reason — modifying 'likes') *who will not read anything complicated* (subordinate adjective clause — modifying 'public').

6 Paragraphs

In our progression from smallest to largest units of writing, we have progressed from *words* through *phrases* and *clauses* to *sentences*. So far we have been concerned with structures in English. Now we are concerned with organisation. We have to organise sentences so that they will clump together in unified groups. These organised clumps of sentences are called **paragraphs**.

Paragraph construction

A paragraph is a unit of thought, not of length. It should deal with only one main idea from all the ideas that come under your topic. The main idea is contained in a topic sentence which itself contains the guiding idea. The topic sentence is usually placed first in the sentence, but experienced writers may choose to place it in the middle or anywhere else to create a desired effect. We will stick to the 'topic sentence first' pattern because it is the simplest both for the writer and the reader. Business people do not have time to figure out your writing pattern, paragraph by paragraph — they appreciate consistency.

The guiding idea points the way to what the reader can expect in the supporting sentences of the paragraph. These sentences supply the evidence in support of the guiding idea. They must stick to the point, however tempting it may be to drag an extraneous comment in. They must not be 'padding' either — if you only have one or two things to write in a paragraph, then one or two sentences will suffice.

Linking words

A paragraph should be a cohesive unit, held together with appropriate links. There are many devices you can use to ensure smooth transition from one sentence to the next and to ensure that the pattern is maintained throughout the paragraph. Transitional devices should tie your thoughts together, guide the reader from one point to the next, and tie the whole paragraph together. They should also link one paragraph to the next, so that all the paragraphs together form a logical presentation of your whole subject. They show various relationships between the things they are connecting. Here are a few you could consider:

- To show addition:
  also, furthermore, in addition

- To illustrate:
  for example, for one thing, for another
- *To show result:*
  accordingly, therefore, as a result
- To show contrast:
  however, nevertheless, on the other hand
- To show sequence:
  next, then, finally or *first, second, third* or *firstly, secondly, thirdly*
- To emphasise:
  indeed, in fact

There are many such transitional devices. Be consistent in your use of them. Remember, you are writing for a reader — your job is to make the reader's job as easy as possible. Signposting your intentions throughout your paragraphs is one way to help the reader. *Repetition* is another way to keep a paragraph on track, or, indeed, to link paragraphs:

- Repeating key words or phrases:

  It was the *courage* of the firemen that was so noticeable. Their *courage* took them into places where less *courageous* people would not go........

- Repeating the subject of the sentence:

  The people will decide what is right. *The people* have always made their choices independently of government. *The people* are directly affected by the outcome of this debate, so it is *the people* to whom we must answer in the long run.

Here is a paragraph which illustrates the points we have just looked at:

Topic sentence guiding idea: *difficulty*	You may have some *difficulty* in writing a paragraph. First of all, think about the idea you want to get across. Second, write a sentence that expresses that idea. Third, think about and write down the ideas that support that idea.
Supporting sentences: suggestions for over- coming difficulty	Finally, write the paragraph, making sure that the sentences are tied together neatly with transitional devices like the ones used here — first of all, second, third etc. Writing a para-
Final sentence ties it together and points to guiding idea in next paragraph.	graph *will not be difficult* if you *approach it systematically.* A *systematic approach* to paragraphing a whole document pays off ...

Suppose you have been asked to report briefly on the job you are about to leave and to recommend improvements that could be put into effect for the benefit of your successor. You might want to discuss working conditions, training and job satisfaction. Let's look at one of those sections: training. This is a big subject and there would be several topics you would want to touch on under that heading — perhaps courses, on-the-job training and release for university study. Each of these could form the germ of an idea for a paragraph. Let's consider just one — courses.

> It has been beneficial both to me and to the department to send me on work-related courses.

Here is a topic sentence we could use to begin the paragraph. What is the guiding idea in this sentence? ..... been beneficial both to me and to the department.....

The supporting sentences should stay on the track dictated by the guiding idea. No extraneous information should be allowed to creep in.

> It has been beneficial both to me and to the department to send me on work-related courses. I have benefited by becoming more aware of the skills needed to further my career. *Also*, I have learned some new skills, particularly in the area of written communication. I am sure my written work is now more accurate and readable than it was beforehand, and this is the main benefit to the department. *In addition*, I find I am able to help other members of the section with their written work. *This*, in turn, has helped me to develop supervisory skills. The benefits of undertaking work-related courses far outweigh the disadvantages of occasional absence from the workplace.

Notice that the sentences are in a logical order, following the order of the guiding idea, and that they are linked by connectives (*also, in addition*), and by use of the pronoun (*this*). Key words (*skills, written*) are repeated. Notice too that the final sentence ties it all together by restating the idea of the first sentence, as well as providing a clue to the topic of a possible second paragraph, 'The disadvantages of occasional absence'.

Exercises

Suppose you have to write a second paragraph to follow the above example. Here is a topic sentence to give you an idea:

> My colleagues have had to put up with a few difficulties while I have been attending courses.

What is the guiding idea of this sentence? What supporting ideas would you suggest including? How would you tie the whole paragraph together in the final sentence?

1 Write the paragraph. When you have finished, make sure that it fits with the first paragraph (above) and that the two together say something cohesive about that one aspect of the report — courses.

2 Re-arrange the following sentences so that they make a logical paragraph. You do not have to alter any words, as the appropriate transitional devices are already there.
   a Then I had to go back to the office because I had left my wallet there.
   b In the end it was 7.30 pm before I reached my home.
   c First, I worked late to finish a report that was due the next morning.

d At last, I got to the bus stop in the main street just in time to see the bus disappearing round the corner.

e I was very late home yesterday, but it wasn't entirely my fault.

3 Here are some more topic sentences. Plan and write a paragraph based on each one (no solutions given):
  • There are only two ways to get slim.
  • Paragraph-writing should be taught in school for these reasons.
  • Drugs can have harmful effects on the human body.

4 Here are two guiding ideas (they are not topic sentences):
  • Reasons for redesigning a/my job.
  • A moment I will always remember.

Write at least two paragraphs based on either of these ideas. Make sure that each paragraph follows the pattern suggested above and that the first and second paragraphs are linked appropriately.

Suggested solutions

1 Possible partial solution:
Guiding idea: a few difficulties
Suggested supporting ideas: 1: remaining staff overworked; 2: jealousy among remaining staff; 3: cranky boss ; 4: work piles up on my desk
Final sentence idea: Despite difficulties (reflecting para 2), there are many advantages (reflecting para 1). Overall, course attendance has been beneficial both to participant and department (tying it all together)
2 e, c, a, d, b
3 and 4: no solutions provided

Two very important questions about paragraphs remain unanswered:
• How long should a paragraph be?
• How many paragraphs make a document?

How long should a paragraph be?

This depends very much on the complexity of the subject matter. Often you need to write quite a lot about one small point in order to make yourself clear. On the other hand, often you need only write a couple of sentences. Paragraphs are any length, from one sentence upwards. In business documents, our aim is to write so that the document will be as readable as possible, and one way to make a document readable is to give the reader small chunks of information at a time. It therefore stands to reason that paragraphs which are shorter rather than longer will be more acceptable. For most business writing, an average of three sentences, with a range of one to six sentences, seems to be easy enough to cope with. Avoid a succession of similar looking paragraphs — paragraphs that all seem to be the same length cause the reader to switch off because of the monotony.

How many paragraphs make a document?

As few as possible, and as many as necessary. If you plan your document carefully, and avoid dragging extraneous information into it, the number of paragraphs will work out automatically.

If you are writing a complex document, you will probably want to signpost your paragraphs for the reader. You can use a hierarchical numbering system and side headings to guide the reader's eye from section to section. It is not necessary to give a heading to every paragraph; side headings should refer to what is to follow in the next block of paragraphs.

7 Punctuation

When you talk to someone face to face, you use facial expression, gestures, pauses, intonation and stress to make your meaning clear. The words alone are not enough. When you talk to someone on the phone, you are limited to pauses, intonation and stress. Have you noticed how important these aids become when you and the other person cannot see each other? When you write, you have none of these aids; something has to take their place. We use punctuation for this purpose, and indicate it with punctuation marks, which are graded according to their function and their importance. Here is a summary of how to use all the punctuation marks we use in English.

Capitals

While not strictly punctuation, the use of capital letters is included here because capitals are signposts that tell the reader that this is something special. You do not use them in speech, but they are necessary in writing and are used:

- at the beginning of a sentence. Every sentence in English begins with a capital letter. This, with the full stop, tells the reader that a new thought is being written about;
- at the beginning of proper nouns, proper adjectives and titles attached to names;
- for the pronoun 'I' but no other pronouns unless they also happen to begin a sentence;
- at the beginning of important words in titles of books etc;
- at the beginning of days of the week, months, special events — but not directions unless they are particular geographical areas like the *Far East*, or seasons unless they are personified as in '*Spring wore a green gown*';
- at the beginning of trade names like *Marmite*, but not for words which have become part of the general vocabulary like *venetian blinds, french windows*;
- at the beginning of the first and last words in the salutation of a letter, and at the beginning of the first word of the closure.

Examples:

> My friend, Mr Armstrong, and I enjoyed reading extracts from *The Merchant of Venice* on Wednesday at the Public Library.

Many senators attended the briefing in Washington, including Senator Wood.

Dear Sir, My dear James, Yours faithfully.

End punctuation

The end of any sentence must be marked by one of the marks : full stop, question mark or exclamation mark. Notice that the question mark and exclamation mark include the full stop on the bottom and so have the same weight as the full stop. Basically, the full stop is used to mark the end of a statement, the question mark at the end of a direct question, and the exclamation mark at the end of a highly emotional statement. The exclamation mark is not used much in business documents except in advertising material. Here are their individual uses.

Full stop

The full stop (sometimes called period) is used

- at the end of a complete statement:
    It is cold in this room because the window is open.
- at the end of a polite request (where a question mark would be inappropriate):
    Please shut the window.
- as a decimal point and to separate hours and minutes:
    The interest rate has fallen to 12.5 per cent.
    The next bus leaves the Hagley Road junction at 3.15 pm.
- at the end of an abbreviation:
    Mr. R. J. Thomas, B.A., Dip.Ed.

It is becoming more common now, however, to omit all punctuation that is not essential. As it is clear that the last example shown here would be perfectly clear without full stops, the current practice is to omit them, and the commas too:

    Mr R J Thomas BA DipEd

Question mark

This mark is only used at the end of a direct question:

    Why haven't you visited our store lately?

Exclamation mark

This mark is only used at the end of a highly emotional sentence or interjection:

    What a magnificent view that is!

    Look out!

    Help!

Comma

This is the most commonly misused, and certainly the most overused, punctuation mark of all. The comma cannot, for example, be used to replace the full stop. You should use appropriate end punctuation to indicate that you have come to the end of a complete thought. Here are the important occasions on which you should use a comma:

• after an initial subordinate clause (but when the main clause is first, no comma is necessary):

> Before the meeting begins, the chairman will make a personal statement.
>
> The chairman will make a personal statement before the meeting begins.

• before and after words in apposition, that is, when two phrases are used side by side, both referring to the same thing. For example:

> John Rogers, the general manager, will address the meeting.
>
> On Friday night, a hazardous time for driving, she crashed her car.

• to separate items in a list, but only before the final *and* if confusion would arise otherwise:

> The salesman showed us some inexpensive, colourful, hand-made articles.
>
> They were instructed to bring pencil, paper, ruler and eraser to the examination.
>
> Those present included the chairperson, the secretary, the team captains and all the members.

Look at this sentence — how many firms are involved?

> The work will be undertaken by Peterson Brothers Abercrombie Jones and Parker and Knight Industries.

The meaning of the sentence can be changed by moving the commas:

> (1) The work will be undertaken by Peterson Brothers, Abercrombie Jones, and Parker and Knight Industries. (3 firms)
>
> (2) The work will be undertaken by Peterson Brothers, Abercrombie, Jones and Parker, and Knight Industries. (4 firms — note that the comma after *Parker* is necessary to separate the firms)
>
> (3) The work will be undertaken by Peterson Brothers; Abercrombie, Jones and Parker; and Knight Industries. (3 firms — different from (1); note that here we have had to use semi-colons to separate the main items in the list because commas already existed in the name of one firm)

• with a co-ordinating conjunction to join two main clauses:

> We did not buy a new car, but we had the old one reconditioned.

• to avoid ambiguity:

> When the chairman finishes the keynote address will begin.
>
> When the chairman finishes, the keynote address will begin.
>
> At night mares cross the road here.
>
> At night, mares cross the road here.

Semi-colon

This punctuation mark is almost as strong as a full stop, but it can also be used when a comma is unavailable. Here are the important occasions on which you should use a semi-colon:

* to join main clauses (without a conjunction):

    We did not buy a new car; we had the old one reconditioned.

* to separate items in a list where commas already appear within items:

    Those present included the chairperson, Jane Abbot; the secretary, Bill Cain; the team captains and all the members.

Colon

There are several uses for the colon in literary writing and in poetry, but we are concerned here with working documents. Here are the important occasions on which you should use a colon:

* to introduce a list:

    Please supply the following:

* to introduce direct speech:

    He said: 'Hello, Joe'.

* to show contrast or balance between two statements:

    To err is human: to forgive divine.

* to introduce an elaboration or explanation:

    The benefits of this new arrangement are twofold: your child will have a wonderful afternoon playing with other children, and you will be free to complete your Christmas shopping in peace.

* to introduce a long quotation:

    In his opening address, the chairman said:

Dash

The single dash is used to indicate a break in thought or an afterthought:

    I had hoped to bring — but that's impossible now.

    There is nothing more I can do for you — it's up to you.

A pair of dashes can be used to enclose an 'aside'; this is illustrated under Parentheses on page 56.

Hyphen

The hyphen is used to divide long words at the end of a line of typing (see page 21 under Spelling).

Hyphenation is also used for the following reasons:

1 To clarify meaning and get rid of any ambiguity.
    For example, in the phrase, *a device used to deice aircraft wings*.
    The word *deice* is likely to be pronounced wrongly, so a hyphen is inserted — *a device used to de-ice aircraft wings*. When someone advertises their

Rolls Royce as *'a little used car'*, they should not be surprised by some of the responses. The expression *'a little used car'* could have two meanings — *'a small car that is not new'* or *'a car that has not been used very much'*, so a hyphen is inserted to show one meaning only: *a little-used car*.

2 To turn two or more words into a compound that is then treated as one word: There are many examples as almost any two words can be combined to form one: *high-flown, steering-wheel, over-indulgent* . One compound that may cause some problems is *up-to-date*. When this compound (and others like it) is used immediately before the noun it modifies, it is joined together as one word with hyphens: an *up-to-date* edition.
When it is after and separated from the noun it modifies, it is written as three separate words:
   This edition is *up to date*.

3 To distinguish between two words having entirely different meanings:
You *recover* from an illness or you *recover* something you lost, but you *re-cover* your lounge suite.

4 To break up combinations of sounds that would be awkward (and probably difficult to pronounce) if left unbroken.
   Where two vowels appear next to each other, it is often advisable to put a hyphen between them to ensure that both vowels will be pronounced : *taxi-ing, semi-invalid, co-occurrence*. However, there are some words which are in constant use which are now being spelt without this hyphen : *co-operation* is becoming *cooperation*. Likewise, where two consonant sounds appear next to each other, it is advisable to put a hyphen between them to ensure that both sounds will be pronounced; *watch-chain* is a good example. Again, there are exceptions — the word *withhold* is spelt without a hyphen although the *th* and following *h* sounds are pronounced separately. You have to decide for yourself whether you think a word is perfectly clear without the hyphen — or not.

5 To mark some common prefixes — but by no means all.
There is no rule about these — check in a dictionary if you are not sure which prefixes are followed by a hyphen. Some that are include *anti-, pro-* and *ex-*, as in *anti-nuclear, pro-Australian, ex-principal*. Some take a hyphen sometimes but not always: *semi-invalid, semicircle, Pre-Cambrian, pre-empt, precursor*. (The spelling is also governed by point 4 above in some of these words.)

6 To write out compound numbers below 100 and to spell out fractions:
thirty-three, ninety-nine and one-quarter, seven-eighths, forty-second, three-thousandths.

Exercise

Rewrite this passage, correcting any faults you can find:

Yesterday I took a chair to the upholsterer and asked him to recover it. He had about thirty five chairs in his work-shop, and I also spotted a little used dresser in a corner. On a table was a copy of yesterdays news-paper and an out of date 'Upholstering Weekly'. He charged me only £25 for the job, which was about one half of other quotes I had been given.

Suggested solutions

> Yesterday I took a chair to the upholsterer and asked him to *re-cover* it. He had about *thirty-five* chairs in his *workshop*, and I also spotted a *little-used dresser* in a corner. On a table was a copy of *yesterday's newspaper* and an *out-of-date* 'Upholstering Weekly'. He charged me only £25 for the job, which was about *one-half* of other quotes I had been given.

Quotation marks

Any direct quote — whether of speech or of someone's writing — should be enclosed in quotation marks (often abbreviated to *quotes*, and sometimes called *inverted commas*). You can use single or double quotes, but the trend is towards using single for the main quotation and double for a quotation within a quotation if necessary.

A straightforward quotation of speech is enclosed in quotes. Any end punctuation which is part of the quotation is inside the quotes.

'Hello, Joe.'

If a final full stop is part of the main sentence as well as part of the quotation, it is placed outside the quotes to indicate that the end of the whole sentence has now been reached. An introduction such as *He said* is usually followed by a colon, but sometimes by a comma, or by nothing at all if the whole sentence is very short.

He said: 'Hello, Joe'.

If the inner and outer sentences are *different* types (eg statement + question, statement + exclamation, question + exclamation), both final stops must be used. In this example, there is a question within a statement, so the question mark must be placed inside the quotes to show that the quoted part is a question and the full stop must be placed outside to show that the main sentence is a statement.

He asked: 'Is that you, Joe?'.

If the inner and outer sentences are the *same* type (eg statement + statement, question + question, exclamation + exclamation), we can dispense with the inner final stop and let the outer one do double duty. In the example below, there is a question within a question. In the first writing, both final question marks are shown. In the second writing, we can see how it should appear when the inner question mark has been eliminated.

(1) Did he ask: 'Is that you, Joe?'?

(2) Did he ask: 'Is that you, Joe'?

When you quote from literature, quote exactly what the author wrote. It helps the reading if short quotations can be incorporated into the sentence:

Palmer's view that 'the wheels of industry are revving up' is shared by many.

Longer quotations look best if they are made to stand out by using smaller print size, wider margins, single line spacing if wider line spacing is used elsewhere, or any combination of these:

> Palmer's view is shared by many. At a recent conference he said:
>
>> 'The wheels of industry are revving up. Support services cannot afford to stay in first gear when technology is already in overdrive'.

If a long quotation is longer than one paragraph, opening quotation marks are used at the beginning of each paragraph, but the closing quotation mark does not appear until the end of the final paragraph. In most cases, quotations must be accompanied by details of the source; to omit these details may leave you open to a charge of plagiarism. There are many ways to present these details depending on the type of material and the context in which it is to appear.

Here is how you deal with a quotation within a quotation where different final stops are needed (question within statement within statement):

> The teacher stopped reading the story at the passage that begins 'Father Bear looked at his empty bowl and growled "Who's been eating my porridge?".'

and this one (exclamation within statement within question):

> Why did the teacher stop reading the story at the passage that begins 'Baby Bear looked at his empty bowl and squeaked "Someone's been eating my porridge and it's all gone!".'?

Of course, it is highly unlikely that you would ever use such complicated punctuation! As a writer of effective English, you would try to cut down on the amount of punctuation, so you would probably re-word the passage:

> The story continued: 'Baby Bear looked at his empty bowl and squeaked "Someone's been eating my porridge and it's all gone!" '. Why did the teacher stop reading there?

Exercise

Try to explain why each of these sentences is punctuated as it is. They are all correct.

1 Did she ask 'What is the time'?
2 Kate said: 'Will you come to see "Giselle"?'.
3 The foreman fumed: 'Why did you ask "When's knock-off time?" when it's only just 9 am now?'.

Solutions

1 Question within question, so let outer question mark serve for both inner and outer.
2 Quotation within quotation (name of artistic work can be shown in quotation marks), so double inside single. Also question within statement, so both question mark and full stop must be shown.

> 3 Question within question but separated, so both question marks must be shown. Also the main sentence is a statement, so a full stop is correct at the very end.

Parentheses

These are interruptions to the construction of the sentence which do not otherwise change it. A parenthetical expression may consist of a word, a phrase, a clause or even a whole sentence.

If it is a very minor break, it is set apart with commas.

> She was, however, unable to attend.

> Our friend, who is on leave, is here.

If it is a stronger break, use dashes.

> He left his job — and for that matter all his old friends — when he returned to Queensland to live.

> The new principal — much to our horror — reintroduced corporal punishment at the school.

If it is stronger still, use curved brackets.

> The noted linguist's lecture (on the phonology of some African languages) bored her audience of non-linguists.

If it is an editorial comment or explanation, use square brackets.

> It was a State funeral [see photograph on page 3] attended by the Prime Minister.

Apostrophe

I have talked about the use of the apostrophe as a mark of possession and as a mark of contraction in the Spelling chapter (see pages 16 and 17). It is important enough to bear repeating here.

Possession

We indicate possession in *nouns* by using an apostrophe immediately after the possessing noun. We only add an *s* after the apostrophe if we need it to make the whole word sound right.

> the shoes of the girl = the girl + ' + s (*girl's*) shoes

> the shoes of the girls = the girls + ' (*girls'*) shoes

> the shoes of the women = the women + ' + s (*women's*) shoes

> the shoes of Peter = Peter + ' + s (*Peter's*) shoes

> the shoes of Charles = Charles + ' + s (*Charles's*) shoes

> the shoes of the actresses = the actresses + ' (*actresses'*) shoes

Possession is not restricted to actual ownership. Look at this sentence:

> We watched the gardener digging up the weeds.

This sentence means that we are watching *the gardener* — we are not primarily watching the digging up of weeds. Suppose we wanted to indicate that we were primarily concerned with *the digging up*. We would have to ask ourselves 'Who is responsible for the digging up?' The only possible answer is 'the gardener'. We would therefore have to show the gardener as the possessing noun:

We criticised the gardener's digging up the new seedlings.

These are difficult constructions for many writers. It is probably easier in practice to avoid them altogether and write:

We criticised the digging up of the new seedlings by the gardener.

We do not use the apostrophe to indicate possession in *pronouns*. Pronouns have their own case system, including a possessive case. The most commonly used possessive pronouns are: my, mine (from *I*); our, ours (from *we*); your, yours (from *you*); his (from *he*); her, hers (from *she*); its (from *it*); their, theirs (from *they*).

Contraction

We indicate contraction by using an apostrophe in place of the omitted letter or letters:

it is : it's (not to be confused with the possessive of *it*, which is *its*)

cannot : can't

we will : we'll

ten of the clock : ten o'clock

Exercise

Punctuate these sentences:

1 She loves classical music big bands and jazz and rock doesnt interest her at all
2 He shouted watch where youre walking for heavens sake as the children neared the cliff
3 The childrens toys and their parents golf clubs havent been packed yet
4 My colleague checking my typing was a great help
5 Is this your signature on the paper entitled butterflies of the south seas
6 Whos application is this [You may need to alter spelling here!]
7 Surely its possible for each task to take its turn isnt it
8 Please meet me at the bank well leave from there at 12 oclock sharp
9 The director asked me to ask you how long you will be away
10 This is your final warning if you are late again you will be dismissed
11 She did well in maths however her english marks were lower than expected
12 All aspects of the case the evidence of the witnesses the behaviour of the defendant and the skill of the prosecutor weighed heavily in favour of a guilty verdict
13 The Harrises farm is at the end of the road
14 She said did you ask what is the time as she turned to face me
15 The meeting was attended by the president Andrew Lloyd the secretary Brian Hobbs the treasurer Jill Packer and thirty members
16 Did he ask Where is the post office

17   Wheres the person whos supposed to check the members identities as they come in
18   While they have a high current income these people have almost none of the real assets found in any prosperous nation the schools hospitals roads banks factories and farms that are the true bases of national wealth

Punctuate these paragraphs:

19   A study has shown that children whose TV viewing was cut back to no more than one hour a day improved their grades in school and seemed happier they played more with other kids and increased their concentration in school one child changed from a passive loner into a friendly playmate
20   Most furniture is expensive clumsy to carry costly to move and uninteresting now there is a move to make your own cheap furniture does not necessarily mean orange crates and constructions of boards on bricks

Suggested solutions

1   She loves classical music, big bands and jazz; and rock doesn't interest her at all.
2   He shouted: "Watch where you're walking, for heaven's sake!" as the children neared the cliff.
3   The children's toys and their parents' golf clubs haven't been packed yet.
4   My colleague's checking my typing was a great help.
5   Is this your signature on the paper entitled <u>Butterflies of the South Seas</u>?
6   Whose application is this?
7   Surely it's possible for each task to take its turn, isn't it?
8   Please meet me at the bank; we'll leave from there at 12 o'clock sharp.
9   The director asked me to ask you how long you will be away.
10   This is your final warning: if you are late again, you will be dismissed.
11   She did well in maths; however, her English marks were lower than expected.
12   All aspects of the case — the evidence of the witnesses, the behaviour of the defendant and the skill of the prosecutor — weighed heavily in favour of a guilty verdict.
13   The Harrises' farm is at the end of the road.
14   She said: 'Did you ask "What is the time?" ' as she turned to face me.
15   The meeting was attended by the president, Andrew Lloyd; the secretary, Brian Hobbs; the treasurer, Jill Packer and thirty members.
16   Did he ask 'Where is the post office'?
17   Where's the person who's supposed to check the members' identities as they come in?
18   While they have a high current income, these people have almost none of the real assets found in any prosperous nation — the schools, hospitals, roads, banks, factories and farms that are the true bases of national wealth.
19   A study has shown that children whose TV viewing was cut back to no more than one hour a day improved their grades in school and seemed happier. They played more with other kids and increased their concentration in school. One child changed from a passive loner into a friendly playmate.
20   Most furniture is expensive, clumsy to carry, costly to move and uninteresting. Now there is a move to make your own. Cheap furniture does not necessarily mean orange crates and constructions of boards on bricks.

8 Some common writing errors

Effective writing does what you want it to do. Assuming that you are familiar with the terminology in the preceding chapters, you will have a reasonable grasp of standard English grammar. To be able to make it work for you, there are certain conventions that you need to observe. One of these is to be comprehensible at first reading.

If your reader has to re-read what you have written in order to make sense of it, you have not written clearly. It is very easy to confuse the reader — think how easily you get confused when you read other people's writing. You might sometimes have to go back because you find that you have read a whole sentence and none of it has made sense. Or you might stumble in the middle of a sentence and wonder how to read the rest because the structure has suddenly changed. In this chapter, we will look at some of the most common ways in which readers can be confused — and at how to clear the problems up.

Parallel and non-parallel structure

Parallel structure means sticking to the same structure for items in any kind of list or series in a sentence. If you write

My uncle enjoys tennis, swimming and to water-ski.

the sentence does not have parallel structure because not all the items in the series it describes have the same structure. *Tennis* and *swimming* are nouns, the names of sports, but *to water-ski* is a verb structure. You could give the sentence parallel structure by changing *to water-ski* to just the name of a sport, *water-skiing:*

My uncle enjoys tennis, swimming and water-skiing.

or you could change *tennis* and *swimming* to the verb forms *to play tennis, to swim*. You would also have to change the verb *enjoys* to *likes to* because in English we cannot say *enjoys to swim:*

My uncle likes to play tennis, to swim and to water-ski.

Look at these examples and see how much easier it is to read the version that has parallel structure than the one that does not.

Sentences lacking parallel structure	Sentences that have parallel structure
It is important to get good marks as well as having fun.	It is important *to get* good marks as well as *to have* fun.
	(Now both items start with to and a verb. Can you think of the other way you could correct the problem? Hint: restructure using present participles, or '-ing' words)
His experience in that dead-end job has made him bitter, sullen and a cynic.	His experience in that dead-end job has made him *bitter, sullen* and *cynical*. (Now all three items are adjectives modifying the pronoun *him*.)
She asked me whether I could do shorthand and my office experience.	She asked me *whether I could do shorthand* and *what office experience I had*. (Now both items are subordinate clauses — previously, the second item was only a noun phrase.)
A vacation job at a seaside motel would give you 1 money for essentials at college, 2 you haven't had a full-time job before, 3 or had time for healthy recreation.	A vacation job at a seaside motel would give you 1 *money* for essentials at college, 2 *experience* in a full-time job, 3 *time* for healthy recreation. (Notice how all three items now begin with the same part of speech — a noun — which naturally follows the verb phrase *would give* and indirect object *you*.)

The last example illustrates a problem which arises when the writer is listing a number of points under an introductory statement. It occurs most often in longer documents such as reports. As the numbered points (or dot points) get more numerous, the writer seems to forget how the main sentence began. Check by adding the second and third items to the introduction:

A vacation job at a seaside motel would give you *you haven't had a full-time job before*.

A vacation job at a seaside motel would give you *or had time for healthy recreation*.

This is the way to test for parallel structure in lists like these. See if the points follow the introduction in a logical sequence.

Exercise

Rewrite each of these sentences observing the conventions of parallel structure.

1 This course teaches you how to plan your subject matter, how to prepare a statement of your thesis, how to support the thesis with several points in well-structured paragraphs, and you then choose an appropriate title.

2 Recycling cans, bottles and cardboard is worthwhile because:
  (a) it re-uses valuable resources,
  (b) prevents piles of rubbish accumulating,
  (c) it has made people aware of the ecology of their environment.
3 There are several careers I am considering, including nursing, teaching
  disabled children, and social work among the homeless.
4 To clean the feed rollers:
  (a) Take out the development unit and place it on a clean sheet of paper.
  (b) Remove the paper tray.
  (c) The rollers should be cleaned with a damp cloth.
5 In my job I have learned to sell and working with many kinds of people.
6 The purpose of the society is to promote understanding between the staff
  and the students and for improvement of the curriculum.
7 The professor warned the new students to be on time, that they should
  follow instructions, and he expected them to be regular in attendance at
  lectures.
8 Under the Act, it is an offence for a person to transfer ownership of a
  company record unless the action is:
  (a) required by another law;
  (b) with the permission of the board of directors;
  (c) in accordance with a normal administrative practice.

Suggested solutions
(there may be others)

> 1 ..... and *how to* choose an appropriate title.
> 2 b it prevents.....
>   c it makes......
>   (that is, use *it* plus *present tense* verbs throughout)
> 3 and do*ing* social work......
>   (three -*ing* forms)
> 4 c *Clean* the rollers with a damp cloth
>   (that is, use the imperative verb throughout)
> 5 .....and *to work* with.....
> 6 .....and *to improve* the curriculum.
> 7 The professor warned the new students to be on time, to follow instructions, and to be
>   regular in attendance at lectures. (There are two other ways to write this sentence in
>   parallel structure. Try to find them.)
> 8 a required by b permitted by c according to (3 verb forms)

Connecting pairs

There is another aspect of parallel structure that is very important. This concerns
the use of *connecting pairs* (or conjunction pairs) like *both....and, either....or,
neither....nor* and *not only....but also*.

When these are used as pairs, it is important to use the right pair — that is, for
example, to make sure that *neither* is followed by *nor* and not by *or*.

Also, it is important to make sure that the two conjunctions are put immediately in front of the words they join.

Max *not only* taught swimming to juniors *but also* to seniors. (incorrect)

Max taught swimming *not only* to juniors *but also* to seniors. (correct)

Parallel structure here means making sure that the structure after each part of the connecting pair is the same.

Exercise

Correct any errors in matching of connecting pairs, and place the parts of the connecting pairs in these sentences so that there is parallel structure:

1 Franz neither is good at maths or at history.
2 Lucy is not only able to do shorthand at 100 words a minute, and typing at 80 words a minute.
3 He likes both cottage cheese and he likes camembert.
4 Grace will compete in either the sprint or in the relay.

Fill in the blanks with appropriate connecting pairs:

5 Looking out of the window was not sufficient to tell _____ it was a warm day _____ not.
6 Her mother is _____ fat _____ thin; she is the right weight for her height.

Solutions

1 Franz is good at neither maths nor history.
2 Lucy is able not only to do shorthand at 100 words a minute, but also to type at 80 words a minute.
3 He likes both cottage cheese and camembert.
4 Grace will compete in either the sprint or the relay.
5 whether/or
6 neither/nor

Shifts in time

Related to parallel structure is keeping a sentence, a paragraph, or even a whole document in the one time throughout — that is, not allowing the tense (time) of the verbs to change from past to present or from present to past. The problem sometimes arises when the writer is relating a story: the story begins in the past tense, telling what happened in the past, but somehow the excitement of the situation is rekindled and the writer seems to want to continue the story in the present as though it were happening all over again. Stick to one or the other, whichever is the more appropriate.

> We *backed* the car into the narrow lane and *waited*. It *wasn't* long before this huge man *emerges* from a doorway. I *tried* to shout but nothing *comes* out.

It could all be in the present or all in the past — which do you prefer?

> We back the car into the narrow lane and wait. It isn't long before this huge man emerges from a doorway. I try to shout but nothing comes out.

Or:

> We backed the car into the narrow lane and waited. It wasn't long before this huge man emerged from a doorway. I tried to shout but nothing came out.

Your preference is dictated by what impression you want to create in the mind of your reader.

Exercise

In these examples, there are shifts in time from present to past or from past to present. Change the verbs in each example to agree with the first verb used.

1 I spent all last week studying for this exam and then they cancel it.
2 Jake worked hard all year, did the exam and wrote a great paper, and only gets a Pass.
3 The meeting opened when the chairperson welcomed everyone. Then she asks the secretary to read the minutes of the last meeting. After that, the meeting was open to new business. Several of us get up to speak at once so the chairperson calls for order. Eventually we all had our say.

Solutions

1 cancelled
2 got
3 asked, got, called

Shifts in person

It is better to write a whole document in one person than to shift from one to another. Very few writers are good enough to get away with a shift of person without allowing the writing to become muddled. Earlier in this book (see page 26) you read that pronouns are grouped according to person:

1st person (person speaking) — *I, we*

2nd person (person spoken to) — *you*

3rd person (person spoken about) — *he, she, it, they*

(and all their various case forms, both singular and plural)

To the 3rd person group, we can add all nouns and the words *one, a person, people, anyone.*

While it is in order to shift from *one* to *he* or *she* because they are all in the same group (3rd person) and are all singular, you should not shift from *one* to *you* or *I*, or from *I* to *you*, because such shifts involve shifting from one group to another.

Most *people* can find work of some kind if *you* are willing to accept anything available. (incorrect)

Most *people* can find work of some kind if *they* are willing to accept anything available. (correct)

When *I* got out of the car, *one* could see that someone else had been here earlier. (incorrect)

When *I* got out of the car, *I* could see that someone else had been here earlier. (correct)

Exercise

Change the pronouns so that there will be no shift in person.

1 All those who want tickets for the concert should have your money ready.
2 I exercise every morning because one can feel it doing you good.

Solutions

1 All those who want tickets for the concert should have their money ready.
2 I exercise every morning because I can feel it doing me good.

Avoiding ambiguity

Ambiguity is uncertainty of meaning. It often occurs in writing because of our efforts to use everyday vocabulary and constructions. Unfortunately, we forget that we cannot show stress, pauses, intonation, etc in writing. If we write exactly as we speak, we risk being unclear. When we write, we must keep the reader in mind all the time. Will this sentence be absolutely clear? Will it have only the one meaning that I intend for the reader? If it is possible to see two (or more) meanings in a sentence, it is ambiguous. Writing ambiguously is not writing effectively because the reader has to ask you to explain what you mean.

There are several types of ambiguity — these are just some of the more interesting types.

Lexical — where a word can have more than one meaning in the context:

She can't *bear* children.

1 She can't have children of her own.

2 She doesn't like children.

The man in the black hat *took* her picture.

1 The man in the black hat is a thief and stole a picture belonging to her.

2 The man in the black hat is a photographer and photographed her.

The *case* is closed.

1 The court case is finished.

2 The suitcase has its lid shut down.

Surface structure — where the meaning changes depending on the stress you put on different parts of the sentence:

I asked how old Barney was.

1 I asked after Barney's health (stress on *how*).

2 I asked what age Barney was (stress on *old*).

She inspected the new students' rooms.

1 She inspected the rooms intended for the new students (stress on *new students*).

2 She inspected the new rooms that have been built for students (stress on *students' rooms*).

The father of Tony and Annabel will arrive tonight.

    1 The man who is father to both Tony and Annabel will arrive tonight (no pause after *Tony*).

    2 Tony's father will arrive tonight with Annabel (pause after *Tony* and add stress to *Annabel*).

Deep Structure — where you have to know what the underlying sentence structure might have been in the speaker's or writer's mind before you can work out the meaning:

Visiting friends can be a nuisance.

    1 It can be a nuisance to have to visit friends.

    2 Friends who visit you may not be welcome at the time.

The hostel caught fire and the residents sought safety in their pyjamas.

    1 The residents were already in their pyjamas and rushed outdoors to safety.

    2 The residents changed into their pyjamas in the belief that wearing pyjamas would make them safe from the fire.

The chicken is ready to eat.

    1 The chicken is cooked, so we can begin to eat it.

    2 The chicken is hungry and will gobble up any food we give it.

Those examples show that it is essential to think carefully about sentences where you use words or structures that are capable of misunderstanding. Never make your reader work out what you mean. Always present the reader with one meaning only. This may result in your writing a slightly longer sentence than you originally intended — so be it. Effective writing is not always the shortest sentence; sometimes you have to use a few more words in order to make your intention quite plain.

Poor reference

Ambiguity can also arise from the incorrect use of pronouns, especially the relative pronoun *which* and the personal pronoun *it*.

    Which:

    The principal asked the teachers to patrol the grounds during the students' demonstration *which* would show that they had the interests of the school at heart.

What does the *which* clause refer to?

• the patrolling of the grounds by the teachers?

• the students' demonstration?

It should refer to whatever immediately precedes it, but in this sentence it could refer to either idea. It would be better to write the sentence again as two sentences:

    The principal asked the teachers to patrol the grounds during the students' demonstration. The students intended to show that they had the interests of the school at heart.

It:

> Jason studied hard at school, came top in English, and went to university to study journalism, encouraged all the time by his family. *It*'s paying off now because his career as a journalist with a major London daily is well under way.

What does *it* refer to? Exactly what is paying off?
- the hard study at school?
- getting top marks in English?
- studying journalism at university?
- family encouragement?

We could write a number of sentences to clear the muddle up — here is just one which relates *it* to the item immediately before it — family encouragement. You might like to try other versions which relate *it* to the other possibilities.

> Jason studied hard at school, came top in English, and went to university to study journalism. His family gave him *constant encouragement* and *it* is paying off now...........

Inadequate punctuation

Ambiguity can also be caused by *inadequate punctuation*. Look at these examples:

1 After the choir and guest soloists finish singing carols including Silent Night will be sung by the congregation.
2 Development of the centre of the city is being speeded up by the city fathers. As the city develops its western sector, complete with its broad avenues of plane trees, will become a focus for recreational pursuits.

In the first example, the reader would naturally read:

> After the choir and guest soloists finish singing carols including Silent Night

before being confronted with a verb *will be sung* for which there has apparently been no subject.

If we put a comma after *singing*, the problem is solved (subject and verb highlighted):

> After the choir and guest soloists finish singing, *carols* including Silent Night *will be sung* by the congregation.

In the second example, the writer has included two essential commas, but has left out one which would make sense of the whole sentence — after *develops*. Without it, the reader again stumbles at the verb *will become* which appears to have no subject.

> Development of the centre of the city is being speeded up by the city fathers. As the city develops, *its western sector*, complete with its broad avenues of plane trees, *will become* a focus for recreational pursuits. (Subject and verb highlighted.)

Exercise

Rewrite these sentences showing their various meanings:

1 He drove the truck as well as his son.
2 Ann gave Meg her hat.
3 He did not go because of what he read in Saturday's paper.
4 The store manager called a meeting of the staff on the office shredder.
5 He found the bat when he opened the cellar door.
6 His father told him he should go without hesitation.
7 I was sorry to hear that she narrowly escaped serious injury.
8 Your supervisor has been asked to look into and report on the disturb-ance and also to comment on the points raised by the workers in their claim which could have a bearing on future negotiations.
9 When the result was announced so promptly, it surprised us all.
10 As soon as the principal finishes the keynote address will be given by Professor Jones.

Solutions

1 (a) Both he and his son drove the truck.
  (b) He drove the truck as well as his son drove it.
2 (a) Ann gave her hat to Meg.
  (b) Ann gave Meg's hat to her.
3 (a) He went, but not because of what he read in Saturday's paper.
  (b) He stayed away because of what he read in Saturday's paper.
4 (a) The store manager called a meeting of the staff on the subject of the office shredder.
  (b) The store manager asked everybody to climb on the office shredder for the meeting.
5 He found (a) a cricket bat OR (b) a flying bat when he opened the cellar door.
6 (a) His father told him he should go and not hesitate.
  (b) His father unhesitatingly told him he should go.
7 (a) I was sorry to hear that she was still alive.
  (b) I am glad she survived.
8 *Which* should refer to *claim*, the closest antecedent, but it could refer to almost anything in the sentence. Here is just one of many solutions:
  Your supervisor has been asked to look into and report on the disturbance and also to comment on the points raised by the workers in their claim. *This claim* could have a bearing on future negotiations.
9 (a) The result, which was announced so promptly, surprised us all.
  (b) The promptness of the announcement of the result surprised us all.
10 Insert a comma after *finishes*:
  As soon as the principal finishes, the keynote address will be given by Professor Jones.

Fragments

A complete sentence must have a subject and a predicate, and the predicate must contain a complete (finite) verb. Even subordinate clauses meet these criteria, so there is one other point to be made about a complete sentence: it can stand alone. To do so, it must be complete in its meaning as well as in its grammatical construction. So we can now say: every complete sentence must contain at least one main clause — otherwise, it is a fragment:

Before the rain started

This has a subject, *rain*, and the finite verb *started*, but it begins with *before*, which is dependent on (subordinate to) a main clause. Because the clause cannot stand alone, it is only a fragment.

> We raked up the fallen leaves

This is a main clause with the subject *we* and the finite verb *raked up*. It stands alone and so forms a sentence. In the examples below, the fragments are given first, followed in each case by the sentences based on them:

1 Disobeyed his parents (has no subject)
He disobeyed his parents. (add subject *he* to complete the sentence).

2 Jill lying in the sun all day long (*lying* is not a complete verb, only a participle)
Jill *was* lying in the sun all day long. (add auxiliary *was* to make complete verb *was lying*)

3 Racing against time (no subject and no complete verb)
Racing against time, *we finished the job with only seconds to spare.* (add a main clause — the original phrase now modifies *we*)

4 The result that everybody expected (no verb for the main clause)
The result [that everybody expected] *was announced* at 9 pm. (add a complete verb for the main clause)

Why shouldn't we use fragments in our writing? After all, we use them in speech. *Every day. Sometimes several times a day.* These last two groups of words are fragments. They seem perfectly all right, and in an informal context they are, but generally they make the meaning less clear.

One context in which fragments might be acceptable is in advertising writing. People who write copy for advertisements are very clever at using language to suit their purpose of selling goods. Another context is in magazines, where journalists try to make stories interesting by sounding chatty. These kinds of fragmented language are, however, not normally acceptable in business writing, so stay clear of them and restrict yourself to complete sentences.

Advertising writers can come unstuck. In their effort to appear chatty, they may neglect those conventions of good writing that make a document readable. Look at this extract from an advertisement calling for entries in a talent quest:

> '.... As well as a great deal of admiration, the winner will also receive two First Class round the world airline tickets. As well as the handsome trophy itself. Send completed forms and as much relevant information (no originals) to ....'

There are three points that we can look at:
1 We do not need to write *also* when we have already written *as well as* to refer to the same idea.
2 *As well as the handsome trophy itself* is a fragment. If it were the only irregularity, it would not matter — it would be accepted as part of chatty advertising writing. (If we want to turn it into a complete sentence, we have to supply a main clause or attach the phrase to the previous sentence so that it can modify *tickets*.)

3 What does the writer mean by *as much relevant information*? As much as what? This leaves the reader up in the air. We need something to complete that connecting pair — the word *as* plus almost anything. Suitable completions would be *as much ... as possible, as much ... as available, as much ... as you can provide*.

Let us try a rewrite:

> '.. As well as a great deal of admiration, the winner will receive two First Class round the world airline tickets. These are in addition to the handsome trophy itself. Send completed forms and as much relevant information as you can provide (no originals) to ....'

It is now at least written in correct English, and it has a better chance of attracting entrants to the competition.

Exercise

For the first group, decide whether the clauses are main clauses or fragments. Put a full stop at the end of any sentence. If the clause is a fragment, add a main clause to make a complete sentence.

1 Whenever they are ready to leave for the picnic races
2 If only I had studied harder
3 There is always something of interest in a big city
4 Come here quickly
5 Which he refused to do

The next group consists of fragments only. Identify what is missing. Write them out again, adding whatever is necessary to turn them into complete sentences.

6 Began at the beginning and went on until the end and then stopped
7 A young mother trying to lift a pram into a bus
8 Running instead of walking along the college corridors
9 Training that you can only get on the job working alongside a colleague
10 Plain English that says what we want to say as concisely and clearly as possible

Suggested solutions

F = Fragment   S = Sentence
1 (F); we will go.
2 (F); I might have passed my exams.
3 (S);(add full stop)
4 (S); (add full stop) (The subject of this sentence is *you* 'understood'.)
5 (F); His mother asked him to empty the garbage bins, ...
6 *He* began at the beginning and went on until the end and then stopped. (add subject)
7 A young mother *was* trying to lift a pram into a bus. (add auxiliary to complete verb)
8 .... corridors, *you will have an accident*. (add complete main clause)
9 *Training* that you can only get on the job working alonside a colleague *is invaluable*. (add verb and complete main clause)
10 *Plain English* that says what we want to say as concisely and clearly as possible *is the best form of writing for business*. (add verb and complete main clause)

Dangling and misplaced modifiers

A modifier is anything that alters the meaning of something else in the sentence. It does it by limiting, describing or emphasising the thing it modifies. Adjectives and adverbs are modifiers:

> The *young* man ran *quickly* to the station.

Young is an adjective modifying *man* and *quickly* is an adverb modifying *ran*.

Modifiers can be much longer than one word — they can be whole phrases or clauses:

> He wore a comfortable tracksuit of grey wool as he lounged in the country house that he shared with his sister.
>
> *of grey wool* — phrase modifying tracksuit
> *country* — adjectival noun modifying house
> *that he shared with his sister* — clause modifying house

When the modifiers are placed correctly, as they are in this example, they provide depth and colour to an otherwise ordinary statement. If, however, the modifiers are not placed correctly, the sentence becomes confusing:

> He wore a comfortable tracksuit of grey wool as he lounged in the house in the country that he shared with his sister.

Does he share the *house* or the *country* with his sister? Modifiers must be placed precisely; otherwise they distort the meaning of the sentence.

Dangling modifiers

Modifers 'dangle' when there is no word to which they can clearly relate. Let us look at some examples:

> Having arrived at home, the door slammed behind him. (the *door* didn't arrive)
>
> Our holiday passed happily, swimming and walking. (the *holiday* didn't swim or walk — we did)
>
> While turning the page, her coffee spilt on the book. (*she* turned the page — not the coffee)
>
> Patrick kept watching the traffic light till green. (*Patrick* didn't turn green — the light did)

Solutions to these could be:

> After he arrived at home, the door slammed behind him.
>
> We had a happy holiday, swimming and walking.
>
> As she turned the page, she spilt her coffee on the book.
>
> Patrick kept watching the traffic light until it turned green.

Misplaced modifiers

Modifiers are misplaced when they are not clearly connected to the thing they are meant to modify. They are not missing but simply in the wrong place. When *adverbs* are misplaced, they cause ambiguity because they can be seen to be attached to either the word before or the word following:

People who teach *rarely* get rich.

Does this mean that people who do very little teaching get rich? Or does it mean that people who teach are unlikely to get rich? The modifier *rarely* should be placed so that only one meaning is possible:

Rarely do people who teach get rich.

We have already seen how the word *only* can be placed almost anywhere in a sentence and thus alter the meaning (see page 32).

Here are some more examples of misplaced modifiers:

The teacher kept the child who was naughty in the corner. (*in the corner* should modify *kept*, not *naughty*)

I located the problem with my TV in the shed. (*wth my TV* should modify problem, not appear to be attached to *in the shed* or to look back to *located;* the TV is not working — I am not using the TV as a tool to locate a problem)

The face of the woman behind the counter which was as expressionless as something carved from marble broke into a welcoming smile when she recognised me. (the *which......* clause seems to modify *counter* whereas it should modify *face*)

Some solutions to these could be:

Because the child was naughty, the teacher kept her in the corner.

In the shed I soon found out what was wrong with my TV. (a total rewrite is often necessary)

Behind the counter was a woman whose face was as expressionless as something carved from marble. When she recognised me, her face broke into a welcoming smile.

Exercise

Correct the 'dangling' and 'misplaced' modifier situations in these sentences:
1 Working too hard and earning too little, my ulcer is playing up again.
2 Before leaving for the United States, a new visa will have to go into my passport.
3 Although starving, fish and wild berries were not his idea of a good meal.
4 Perched on her head, he couldn't help noticing her feathered cocktail hat.
5 Waving frantically, the taxi went right past me.
6 In the quiet of the countryside I could hear the rooks in the distant trees that were cawing.

Suggested solutions

1 Because I have been working too hard and earning too little, my ulcer is playing up again.
2 Before I leave for the United States, I will have to get a new visa.

3 Although he was starving, he did not look forward to a meal of fish and wild berries.
4 He couldn't help noticing the feathered cocktail hat perched on her head.
5 The taxi went right past me although I waved frantically.
6 In the quiet of the countryside I could hear the rooks that were cawing in the distant trees.

Lack of subject-verb agreement

The verb in a sentence must agree with its subject in number. That is, if the subject is singular, the verb must be singular; if the subject is plural, the verb must be plural. There is usually no problem when the subject and verb are close to each other and in the normal word order (subject then verb). Problems arise when prepositional phrases come between subject and verb, when the subject and complement of an equational sentence are different in number, when there is a compound subject, and when we are dealing with collective nouns. Let us look at each of these situations:

A box of apples (was/were) delivered this morning. (*was* is correct because the true subject is *box*; the prepositional phrase that modifies it has no bearing on the verb)

The topic of his lecture (is/are) his experiences in the South Seas. (*is* is correct because, in an equational sentence — one where the subject and the material following the linking verb are the same thing — the verb takes its number from the subject)

John and his brother (has/have) arrived. Here (comes/come) John and his brother. (plural *have* and *come* are correct in both — the word order makes no difference.)

Egg and bacon (is/are) my favourite breakfast. (*is* is correct because egg-and-bacon in this context is considered as one unit)

Mary, along with her three children, (was/were) travelling to Sydney. (*Was* is correct. When a singular subject is followed by words or phrases meaning *with* or *as well as,* a singular verb follows.

Neither the boy nor the girl (cares/care) what happens. (*cares* — singular)

Neither the boys nor the girl (cares/care) what happens. (*cares* — singular)

Neither the boy nor the girls (cares/care) what happens. (*care* — plural)

(In the last three sentences, the verb takes its number from the nearer noun; this applies to *either...or, neither...nor, not only...but also* and *or* situations.)

Neither of the children (wants/want) to go to the circus. (*Wants* is correct here. In this situation, *neither* is a pronoun acting alone, without *nor*, and is singular. Other singular pronouns include *anyone, everybody, someone, each* — there are more.)

Exercise

Choose the correct form of the verb in brackets:

1 The cause of sunspots (is/are) well known to scientists.
2 Two aircraft of the VIP fleet (is/are) missing.
3 The main problem on the picnic (was/were) the hundreds of flies.
4 Candlelight and good wine (adds/add) a touch of romance to an evening.
5 Neither the teachers nor the student (believes/believe) his parents are at fault.
6 Canberra, along with many other capital cities, (is/are) being considered as a venue.
7 Everybody at the conference (knows/know) what to do in an emergency.
8 Each of the tomatoes in the crates on the shelves (has/have) been sprayed.

Solutions

1 is; 2 are; 3 was; 4 add; 5 believes; 6 is; 7 knows; 8 has.

Lack of pronoun-antecedent agreement

A pronoun often relates to a word which appeared earlier in the sentence and which is called the antecedent of the pronoun. The pronoun should represent the antecedent accurately, so it should be the same in number, person and gender. This is not difficult, provided gender is quite clear. Here are some examples:

The headmaster arrived in the classroom wearing *his* academic gown. (*his* agrees with *headmaster* — both are singular, 3rd person and masculine)

The chief bridesmaid is responsible for the beautiful flowers which came from *her* own garden. (*her* agrees with *bridesmaid*)

The children will have *their* tea now. (*their* agrees with *children*)

However, sometimes gender is not clear. It is no longer enough to say that, in order to avoid the clumsy *he or she* (or the worse *s/he*) when we need a gender-free, singular 3rd person pronoun, we should use the masculine pronouns *he* and *him* except where the antecedent is clearly feminine. In addition, it is not nowadays possible to assume that the context of a sentence indicates the gender of the participants. It is plainly tactless, for example, to write sentences like these:

Each of the students wants to have *his* say in the tutorial. (A group of students is often made up of men and women, and sometimes women predominate — not necessarily the other way around.)

Every member of the nursing team must pull *her* weight. (There are more and more male nurses these days — in some areas males predominate.)

So what are we to do? I suggest we return to a construction that was in use in the English of several centuries ago — where necessary use **'singular they'**. (See also page 26.) If someone leaves an umbrella behind at the end of a course, the teacher doesn't call out after the group: 'Hey! Someone has left *his or her* umbrella behind'. Instead, the most natural thing to say is: 'Hey! Someone has left *their* umbrella behind'. So we could write:

Each of the students wants to have *their* say in the tutorial.

Every member of the nursing team must pull *their* weight.

Some grammarians will say that this is a colloquialism that should not be carried across from speech to writing. In this instance I disagree. Speech is the forerunner of writing and cultural changes precede both. Our culture now deplores discrimination on grounds of gender; our speech already reflects our cultural standpoint; it is only a matter of time before all writing catches up. It is pointless to go on insisting that *he* is an appropriate pronoun to use when everyone knows that it is inaccurate. You still have the option of recasting the sentence in the plural if you prefer:

All of the students want to have *their* say in the tutorial.

All the members of the nursing team must pull *their* weight.

You will have to resolve this interesting topic for yourself. English is a living language and therefore changing all the time. What was unacceptable yesterday becomes acceptable today. In a situation where cultural values have changed rapidly, language change is sometimes speeded up. Meantime, we all have to write effectively to people who may or may not go along with our views. Consider your reader and then decide what is appropriate.

Exercise

Correct the use of pronouns in these sentences where necessary:
1 Neither of the trees will shed their leaves until the autumn.
2 The company moved into their new office last week.
3 Each of the tomatoes in the crates on the shelves had black spots on them.
4 Either Angie or Rebecca will have to give up their seat.
5 Neither Martin nor Prue took their notes home.

This group provides practice in agreement of subject and verb, as well as pronoun and antecedent. Choose the correct word from the words in brackets:
6 Many a man and woman (has, have) been keen to advance (himself, herself, themselves).
7 Strawberries and cream (is, are) my favourite summer dessert.
8 (We, us) students have to stick together.
9 Neither the boys nor Mr Peterson (know, knows) what (he, they) (is, are) to do next.
10 The audience (was, were) restless, and (it, they, he, she) soon began stamping (his, her, its, their) feet on the floor.

Suggested solutions

1 its leaves; 2 its office; 3 on it; 4 her seat; 5 I would allow *their* as correct, but you could recast the sentence to read: Both Martin and Prue left their notes behind.

6 *Many a* is a singular expression, so we have to use *has* and then we have a problem. It would be better to recast the sentence using *Many* which is plural: Many men and women have been keen to advance themselves.

7 *Strawberries and cream* functions as a single unit, so *is* is the correct verb.

8 *We students* (subject of sentence)

9 *knows, he, is* (agreement with the second item which is singular)

10 *Audience* is a collective noun so we first have to decide whether (like the jury) the word is to be considered as people acting as a whole unit or acting as separate individuals. A singular construction throughout leads to problems. It is better to regard them as separate individuals and so use the plural: The audience were restless, and they soon began stamping their feet on the floor. Another solution is to regard *audience* as singular in the first part and plural in the second. So one way of re-writing the sentence would be: The audience was restless. They soon began stamping their feet on the floor.

Comma fault and run-on sentences

This is the habit of some writers of using a comma where there should really be a full stop, or at least a semi-colon. When you come to the end of a complete thought, you have to indicate it by using stronger punctuation than a comma.

Thank you for your letter, your order will reach you soon. (incorrect)

Thank you for your letter. Your order will reach you soon. (correct)

Related to the comma fault is the practice of stringing sentences together with the comma + conjunction when they are really not closely related. The practice results in some quite long sentences.

She was a good student at school, achieving high grades in all subjects, and I like her because she is fun to be with. (incorrect)

She was a good student at school, achieving high grades in all subjects. I like her because she is fun to be with. (correct)

Misuse of part of speech (eg adverb)

Adverbs modify verbs etc; they cannot be used as nouns or noun clauses.

Didn't he say where he hated taking medicine? (incorrect)

Didn't he say that he hated taking medicine? (correct)

Where makes the clause *where he hated taking medicine* appear to be an adverbial clause of place. *That* makes it a noun clause and the direct object of the verb *did...say*.

Omission of essential verb

When the subject and verb of each clause of a sentence are the same in number (singular or plural), and the verb is the same in each clause, you can avoid unnecessary repetition by omitting the second verb, thus:

My mother plays tennis and my father cricket.

It is permissible to omit *plays* after *father* in this construction as *mother* and *father* are both singular and the verb would be exactly the same. However:

My mother plays tennis and my brothers and sisters cricket. (incorrect)

My mother plays tennis and my brothers and sisters play cricket. (correct)

Revision exercise

Here is a comprehensive exercise on points of grammar and sentence structure. You may wish to regard it as a post-test and compare your results with those of the pre-test on page 8, so the solutions are all together at the end of the exercise.

Part A Parts of Speech

1 Underline the *nouns* in the following sentences:

        eg   Mary had a little <u>lamb</u>.

(a) The audience at the concert heard a symphony by Beethoven and several arias from Tosca.

(b) Tennis is good exercise.

2 Underline the *pronouns* in the following sentences:

(a) She will give it to her friend whose promotion they're celebrating.

(b) This is my book, but I don't know whose that is.

3 Underline the *verbs* or *verb phrases* in the following sentences. Also label each as *active* (A) or *passive* (P).

(a) Please read the instructions carefully unless they have already been read to you.

(b) Your application has been rejected but you can apply again next year.

4 Underline the *adjectives* or *adjective phrases* in the following sentences.
Also label each as *positive* (P), *comparative* (C) or *superlative* (S).

(a) This test is hard, but it's no worse than the old test which was harder than the earliest one.

(b) The slowest way home is often the most beautiful.

5 Underline the *adverbs* in the following sentences:

(a) My dog eats quickly when he is very hungry.

(b) They sat quite quietly and waited to hear who had gained the highly sought-after prize.

6 Underline the *prepositions* in the following sentences.
Also draw a circle around the whole *prepositional phrases*.

(a) Under the table was the cat, curled up in his basket.

(b) Do you think Peter would come with us if we said we would take him to the concert?

7 Underline the *conjunctions* in the following sentences:

(a) Unless you hurry, you will miss the fireworks and the pageant because they have begun.

(b) I must finish this report quickly, but the letters can wait or someone else can do them.

Part B Sentences or Fragments

Say whether the clauses that follow are *fragments* (F) or *sentences* (S). If there are any *fragments*, add to the beginning or end whatever words are necessary to make them into *sentences*. (Do not alter the wording of these clauses.)

1 While he understood perfectly what the lecturer was saying
2 Because they still had more work to do she and Mary together without any help from their fellow workers
3 Look out down there
4 If I studied harder and spent more time working on the assignments that are set
5 After I came home from work on that very hot day when the plants in the garden were crying out for a drink and my body ached for a long cool shower

Part C Check of Some Areas of Spelling, Grammar, Sentence Structure and Basic Punctuation

There are several errors in each of these sentences. Make all necessary corrections. (Do not alter words or word order unless necessary.)

1 He has been quiet successful, each of his trophys are displayed in it's proper place on the shelf.
2 Working hard last term my grades in social studies mathematics and english improved.
3 Yes personally I think Jo's costume is more attractive than Rob and should of won a prize.
4 The choir sang a nonsense song in the variety concert which was full of surprises.

Part D Sentence Structure Exercise

Identify the *main* fault (there may also be minor faults) in each sentence and then rewrite the sentence correctly. There are no spelling errors in these sentences.

1 To a golfer, a hole-in-one means a lot of practice over many years. Also the happiness that the successful golfer feels.
2 There was bad news today for smokers, from now on they must not smoke in offices.
3 I heard where you are thinking of swimming in the Institute pool again.
4 Each of the sisters have their own room which they have decorated according to their own taste.
5 Wally Masur is one of the best tennis players Australia has ever produced, and he grew up and went to school in Canberra.
6 Angela was the best English student in her class at school, which is one of the top schools in Edinburgh, and she came from a family who encouraged her to do well in everything, and it's paying off now because she is making a lot of money from freelance journalism.
7 The car is clean but the bicycles belonging to Katy and Todd still dirty.
8 This free sample packet of Sudsy has been sent to you with our good wishes which we trust will make washing up a more pleasant chore.
9 Speaking at Miss Johnson's farewell party, Mr Jones said that she always worked well, helped her colleagues, and never failed to attend staff meetings.
10 The company needs typists, receptionists and people to sell.

Solutions

Part A

1 (a) audience, concert, symphony, Beethoven, arias, Tosca; (b) tennis, exercise
2 (a) she, it, her, whose, they; (b) this, my, I, whose, that
3 (a) read (active) have...been read (passive); (b) has been rejected (passive), can apply (active)
4 (a) hard (positive), worse (comparative), old (positive), harder (comparative), earliest (superlative); (b) slowest (superlative), most beautiful (superlative)
5 (a) quickly, very; (b) quite, quietly, highly
6 (a) under (under the table), in (in his basket); (b) with (with us), to (to the concert)
7 (a) unless (subordinating), and (co-ordinating), because (subordinating); (b) but (co-ordinating), or (co-ordinating)

Part B

1 (F)... he seemed to be unable to answer the questions.
2 (F)... kept going until they finished.
3 (S)[Just add an exclamation mark]
4 (F)... I would probably pass my exams.
5 (F)... I discovered that the air conditioner had broken down.

Part C

1 He has been quite successful. Each of his trophies is displayed in its proper place on the shelf.
2 Because I worked hard last term, my grades in social studies, mathematics and English improved.
3 Yes, I think Jo's costume is more attractive than Rob's and should have won a prize.
4 The choir sang a nonsense song, which was full of surprises, in the variety concert. OR The choir sang a nonsense song in the variety concert. The concert was full of surprises.

Part D

1 (second string of words is a fragment)
To a golfer, a hole-in-one means a lot of practice over many years as well as happiness at the success.
2 (comma fault)
There was bad news today for smokers. From now on they must not smoke in offices.
3 (misuse of adverbial construction)
I heard that you are thinking of swimming in the Institute pool again.
4 (non-agreement: singular subject *each* takes singular verb and singular pronoun)
Each of the sisters has her own room which she has decorated according to her own taste.
5 (two unrelated thoughts)
Wally Masur is one of the best tennis players Australia has ever produced. He grew up and went to school in Canberra.
6 (very long because of both embedded clauses and add-ons; poor reference of *it*)
Angela was the best student of English in her class at school which was one of the top schools in Edinburgh. She came from a family who encouraged her to do well in everything. Angela's success at school is paying off now because she is making a lot of money from freelance journalism.
7 (omission of essential verb)
The car is clean but the bicycles belonging to Katy and Todd are still dirty.
8 (poor reference)
This free sample packet of Sudsy has been sent to you with our good wishes. We trust it will make washing up a more pleasant chore.
9 (non-parallel and negative)
Speaking at Miss Johnson's farewell party, Mr Jones said that she always worked well, helped her colleagues, and attended staff meetings.
10 (non-parallel)
The company needs typists, receptionists and salespersons.

9 Plain English expression and style

If we wrote everything in correct English, according to the conventions of currently acceptable grammar, our writing would be just that — grammatically correct.

Did you know that it is perfectly possible to write grammatically correct English and not be understood? Perhaps you think that that is a contradiction in terms? Perhaps you think that grammatically correct English is automatically understandable. Nothing could be further from the truth. Of course, it is possible to write grammatically correct sentences that are also perfectly plain, but such sentences are not as common as they should be.

Did you understand the first sentence in this chapter? You probably did because I tried to make sure that it was both grammatically correct and understandable. Look at the next sentence and see if you think it is just as understandable:

> In the event that everything that is written is written in faultless English, according to the conventions of grammar that are acceptable at this point in history, the writing performed would be precisely according to expectation — error-free in every grammatical detail.

That sentence is grammatically correct, but it is hard to understand for several reasons:

- It is much longer than the original.
- It uses passive instead of active verbs; this has the effect of making it possible to leave out the agent (the doer of the action), so we cannot tell who is responsible for anything.
- It uses the lifeless verbal noun *expectation* instead of the lively verb *expect*.
- It uses words and phrases that are long-winded or that are not as familiar to most readers as some others — for example, *faultless* instead of *correct,* and *in the event that* instead of *if.*

Does it matter that the sentence is long and passive, uses verbal nouns and some long-winded phrases? Pick up any of the novels of a classic author such as Charles Dickens and you will see that many of the sentences are constructed just like that. That is fine when you have plenty of time to curl up in a comfortable chair and read for the pleasure of becoming involved in poetic description of scenes from a past age.

In our working lives we do not have the luxury of unlimited time for reading. A working document must be crystal clear to the audience to whom it is addressed, and it must be clear at first reading. Your writing must therefore be grammatically correct; it must observe the rules about using parallel construction, about avoiding ambiguity and about dodging all the writing traps that can cause confusion for the reader. On top of these, your writing, if it is to be absolutely plain, must take account of some features that we have not yet mentioned — aspects of writing that are referred to when people discuss plain English style.

In this chapter, we will work on these stylistic aspects of writing by examining some examples of what can happen when plain English constructions are not used, by trying to put matters right so that what is not plain becomes plain, and by providing some exercises for you to try. Most of the material in this part of the book is based on sentences and paragraphs which can and do appear in real business documents. They can occur in both private business and government departments, and in the kinds of documents you read every day in public notices, legal agreements, prospectuses, insurance policies, banking documents, newspaper articles and elsewhere.

It is too easy to blame a few professions for all obscure writing. It is true that lawyers continue to use antiquated expressions and long, involved sentence structures, but at least it is possible to point to historical and interpretive reasons for some legalese. It is not possible to find sound reasons for the same sort of writing in business letters, reports and public information documents produced by junior and middle management in government departments or private industries.

Even when it is possible to see why some people do not write plain English, it is not possible to support its continued use. When we write to each other, we are simply putting on paper what we would have said if we had been able to talk to each other. So why should the language we use for writing be so different from the language we use for talking to each other? There is no reason.

We do not say to a friend: *This is to inform you that your invitation to lunch is accepted. At this point in time, I have to conduct some business, but I will meet you at the restaurant. Trusting this will be convenient.*

This is to inform you that..., at this point in time... Trusting this... Where do they all come from? If you have been working for a few years, cast your mind back to the day your boss first asked you to write a letter or a memo. Chances are that you were too shy or scared to ask for help in writing it, and, having no previous experience, you went to the files to see how someone else wrote letters and memos. Right? And how do you suppose that person learned how to write letters and memos? Right again! The style has been copied for decades — everyone in succession thinking 'If it was all right for them, it must be all right for me'. The upshot is that today's new young managers, clerical assistants and administrative officers are still copying a writing style that could be anything up to half a century out of date. It is quite possible that the style was something like spoken English at first — it is nothing like it now. A primary aim in writing should be to write in language that is as near as possible to the language we use for speech.

If we use everyday words and sentence structures that we are comfortable with, our readers are likely to be comfortable with them too. This is important when documents are used to inform other people, especially those who are not good readers. Because words and structures that we would not dream of using in speech make writing stilted and convoluted, people who have difficulty in reading will fail to understand straight away what they have to do.

Here is an example of a sentence which is intended to explain an important business term to ordinary people like you and me. Read it through quickly first and then re-read it to discover the grammar of it. You will find that it is perfectly correct according to the conventions of grammar that we have discussed.

'Account Statement' means a printed statement setting out the essential details of those transactions effected on a cardholder's account during the period to which the statement is expressed to refer and of which transactions the Company is aware, together with such adjustments (if any) as the Company believes are necessary to properly reflect transactions effected during a period prior to that to which the statement is expressed to refer and which were omitted or improperly recorded on the statement for that prior period and such further entries as the Company may pursuant to these Rules be authorised to make.

Why, if it is grammatically correct, is this explanation so complicated? It is because the company is trying to cover all possible loopholes. However, there is no excuse for writing an explanation in such difficult language. There are certain faults that it has in common with the example on page 79:

- It is *too long* for one sentence.
- It uses *passive* verbs.
- There are many *qualifications* of the initial statement, some added on by means of conjunctions and others embedded by means of subordinate clauses.
- It uses *unfamiliar terms* such as 'pursuant'.

We will look at features of style like these in the sections below and in the next chapter.

Sentence length

Long sentences are difficult to read just because they are long. When we read, we read in chunks, and if the writer asks us to read a long chunk, we are likely to forget the beginning of it before we finish reading it. By the time we get to the end of a long sentence, we have lost the beginning and have to re-read it. Perhaps you could argue that, because we read in chunks, we should be breaking material down into chunks that we can easily remember as we go? It doesn't work like that. We are accustomed to the idea that the sentence, from capital letter to full stop, is the meaningful chunk that we are meant to remember; as a result, we go on reading and trying to understand, even when the sentence is too long for us to remember easily.

Sentences become long in two main ways:

1 by a*dding* more information using co-ordinating conjunctions to glue the material together, and

2 by *qualifying* with subordinate clauses either added to or embedded in the main statements of the sentence.

'Added on' sentence

Here are two examples of *'added-on'* long sentences:

Example 1

> Courses for next term will include one-day seminars on stress management, plain English awareness *and* personal development *and* will be held in the small meeting room, *and* there will also be two-day workshop courses on effective writing, effective listening *and* reading, *and* report writing. [44 words]

The first step is to decide where the main ideas are in this sentence. I suggest that there are two main ideas, the first one ending at the words *meeting room*. Without doing anything except put a full stop where the following conjunction is, we straight away have much more readable and understandable sentences:

> Courses for next term will include one-day seminars on stress management, plain English awareness *and* personal development *and* will be held in the small meeting room. There will also be two-day workshop courses on effective writing, effective listening *and* reading, *and* report writing. [26 + 17 words]

There are still some co-ordinating conjunctions highlighted. Can we split the sentences further without losing sense? Yes. Look at the arrangement of information in the first sentence: you will see that the venue mentioned applies to all courses — not just one-day seminars. So the first sentence can be rearranged to make two sentences. The second sentence is already a manageable length, so leave it alone.

> Courses for next term will be held in the small meeting room. They will include one-day seminars on stress management, plain English awareness and personal development. There will also be two-day workshop courses on effective writing, effective listening and reading, and report writing. [12 + 14 + 17 words]

These three shorter sentences are very much easier to take in at first reading than the original long sentence. Any conjunctions still there are essential to the grammar and meaning.

Example 2

> The Regional Service Officer *or* Duty Officer (Management Services) in the case of Head Office *and* where a company vehicle is used, shall arrange for collection of trip sheets *and* subsequent analysis *AND* bring any instances of unauthorised trips *or* other irregularity to the attention of the

> departmental manager nominated as responsible for the allocation, use *and* control of transport. [60 words]

The capitalised co-ordinating conjunction *AND* is the glue which joins the two major chunks of this sentence together. There are other conjunctions, but they are essential ones. Let us see if we can at least split this long sentence into two shorter ones.

Decide where the main ideas of the sentence start and finish. The first main idea here is that the officer has to see that *trip sheets are collected and analysed*. The second main idea is that the same officer has to *report any irregularities* to someone. If we simply split the sentence and give the second sentence a subject, we still have rather unwieldy sentences:

> The Regional Service Officer *or* Duty Officer (Management Services) in the case of Head Office *and* where a company vehicle is used, shall arrange for collection of trip sheets *and* subsequent analysis. [32 words]

> [He will also] bring any instances of unauthorised trips *or* other irregularity to the attention of the departmental manager nominated as responsible for the allocation, use *and* control of transport. [30 words]

This is certainly an improvement, and may be as far as you want to go, but 62 words is too many. We can now rearrange the material to make it shorter and easier still to read, without losing the sense of it:

> Where a company vehicle is used at Head Office, the Regional Service Officer or Duty Officer (Management Services) arranges collection and analysis of trip sheets. [25 words]

> He also reports any irregularity to the departmental manager responsible for allocating, using and controlling transport. [16 words]

This is very much easier to understand. The first sentence is a little long, but only because it contains two long titles which are unavoidable. Can you see how the original sentence has changed, besides being cut into two parts? The subject and verb are together, there is less wordiness, the verbs are active instead of passive and some verbal nouns have become the verbs they were derived from. These stylistic changes will be discussed in the sections that follow.

'Qualified sentence'

Here is an example of a *'qualified'* long sentence:

> For files, general papers, maps and plans *which* are more likely to have to be housed in the supporting data section, I think that it would be useful to include a half a page of notes on each in the library *where* we customarily keep one copy of everything of value, *as well as* a reasonable amount of detail for microfilm, *which* has specific storage requirements for masters in particular. [70 words]

Again, the first step is to separate out the main ideas and write about each one separately. Qualifications and conditions are best written as separate sentences too, where possible. Here is my suggested rewrite of this sentence — of course, you may have different ideas:

> Files, general papers, maps and plans are more likely to have to be housed in the supporting data section. I think that it would be useful to include a half a page of notes on each in the library. We customarily keep one copy of everything of value in the library. We should also include a reasonable amount of details for microfilm. This has specific storage requirements for masters in particular. [19 + 20 + 12 + 11 + 9 words]

You can see that I have used almost the same number of words as were in the original sentence, but we now have five sentences. Notice, too, that there is variation in the length of the sentences. Very short sentences can become boring to read because they often drop into a pattern of length and rhythm. The result is that the reader becomes lulled into a state of inattention. The best grouping of sentences is a mixture of long and short.

Adapting long sentences

Here is an example based on a public notice. It contains both the *added-on* and the *qualified* kinds of lengthening. I wonder how many people would bother to read it right through:

> Would any person *who* on Friday 24 January 19— witnessed the accident between a yellow and blue motor vehicle and a box trailer approximately 5 mls from Hull at approximately 3.00 to 3.15 pm *or* the driver of the truck with the Apex Building Company sign at the front *who* was in the vicinity of the accident on that date *or* any other driver *who* may be able to help identify the driver of the said truck *or* the fact that the truck was in the vicinity at that time please contact Messrs Justice, Scales & Company, Solicitors of Hull on (062) 000 1234. [88 words(approx)]

It would take up very little more room in the paper if it were written as follows (using plain English terms instead of the legalese):

> On Friday 24 January 19—, an accident occurred between a yellow and blue car and a box trailer. It occurred about 5 miles from Hull at about 3.00 to 3.15 pm. Did you see this accident?
>
> Or were you driving an Apex Building Company truck on that date? Such a truck was seen near the accident.
>
> Or can you help identify the driver of the Apex truck? Did you see the Apex truck near the accident?
>
> If you can help, please contact Messrs Justice, Scales & Company, Solicitors, of Hull on (062) 000 1234.
>
> [33 + 20 + 20 + 16 = 89 words (approx)]

Sometimes it is not necessary to alter the wording to make a sentence appear shorter. Look at this sentence:

> The Chairman announced that there had been a profit of £1.5 million and that the directors had decided to spend some of it on new staff amenities — refurbishing the canteen (£10 000), providing a new lounge (£30 000), buying a staff holiday house at the coast (£80 000) and providing univer-

sity scholarships for two staff members (£12 000).

This sentence would be easier to read if the items in the series were *listed* under each other. There is no need to alter the wording at all (except to omit *and*):

The Chairman announced that there had been a profit of £1.5 million and that the directors had decided to spend some of it on new staff amenities:

• refurbishing the canteen	£10 000
• providing a new lounge	£30 000
• buying a staff holiday house at the coast	£80 000
• providing university scholarships for two staff members	£12 000

Even legal documents can be made easier to read. The next example is an extract from a typical legal notice appearing in a daily newspaper. This one concerns an application by an organisation (which I have called Arabella Properties Limited) to the High Court to have their capital reduced:

In The High COURT OF JUSTICE CHANCERY DIVISION MANCHESTER DISTRICT REGISTRY No. 123 of 199– IN THE MATTER OF **ARABELLA PROPERTIES LIMITED** AND IN THE MATTER OF THE COMPANIES ACT 1985 NOTICE IS HEREBY GIVEN that a Petition was on 28th February 199– presented to Her Majesty's High Court of Justice for the confirmation of the cancellation of the Share Premium Account of the above-named Company and the reduction of the capital of the Company from £250,000 to £10,000 by returning capital which is in excess of the wants of the Company AND NOTICE IS FURTHER GIVEN that the said Petition is directed to be heard before The Honourable Mr. Justice Scott Vice-Chancellor of the County Palatine of Lancaster at the Law Courts Crown Square Manchester on Monday the 10th day of April 199– ANY Creditor Shareholder or Stockholder of the said Company desiring to oppose the making of an Order for the confirmation of the said cancellation of the said Share Premium Account and the said reduction of Capital should appear at the time of hearing in person or by Counsel for that purpose. A copy of the said Petition will be furnished to any such person requiring the same by the under-mentioned Solicitors on payment of the regulated charge for the same. DATED this 19th day of March 199– Able, Doughty & Bright of Manchester House, 30 Manchester Street, Manchester M2 7XB Solicitors for the above named company.

To make such documents understandable, you have to translate them, bit by bit. The phrases on the left are from the original document. Those in *italic* are my suggested translations:

IN THE HIGH COURT ...
In the High Court of Manchester, case number 123 for this year

IN THE MATTER OF ...
is about Arabella Properties Limited and the Companies Act 1985.

NOTICE IS HEREBY GIVEN
Note

that a Petition was ...
a request was made to the court on 28 February

for the confirmation of ...
for the court to confirm that the amount of money which the Company has available to spend should be reduced to only what the Company must have

to keep going (so that the rest can be paid out to those people to whom the Company owes money).

AND NOTICE IS FURTHER GIVEN
Also note

that the said Petition ...
that the request is to be heard by Mr Justice Scott (the judge)

at the Law Courts Crown Square ...
at this Court on Monday 10 April 199–.

ANY Creditor Shareholder or Stockholder of the said Company
anyone who is owed money by the Company or has a share in it

desiring to oppose ...
who is against granting the request of the Company

should appear at the time of hearing in person or by Counsel for that purpose.
should come to the court on 10 April or should send a barrister to represent them.

A copy of ...
a copy of the Company's request will be sent by the Company's solicitors (address below) to anyone who asks for it, on payment of the usual fee.

DATED this ...
Dated 19 March 199–, Able, Doughty & Bright, of Manchester House, 30 Manchester Street, Manchester, M2 7XB, Solicitors for the Company.

The full revision is as follows:

In the High Court in Manchester, case number 123 for this year is about Arabella Properties Limited and the Companies Act 1985. Note that a request was made to the court on 28 February for the court to confirm that the amount of money which the Company has available to spend should be reduced to only what the Company must have to keep going (so that the rest can be paid out to those people to whom the Company owes money). Also note that the request is to be heard by Mr Justice Scott at this court on Monday 10 April 199–. Anyone who is owed money by the Company or has a share in it and who is against granting the request of the Company should come to the court on 10 April or should send a barrister to represent them. A copy of the Company's request will be sent by the Company's solicitors (address below) to anyone who asks for it, on payment of the usual fee. Dated 19 March 199–, Able, Doughty & Bright, Manchester House, 30 Manchester Street, Manchester, M2 7XB, solicitors for the Company.

The document could be improved further, but there is a clear difference in the length. When you translate documents in this way, your next step must be to check that the document still means exactly what it meant in the original form. Your aim is not to alter meaning — just to make the document plainer.

Another problem that arises when sentences become too long is that essential parts of the sentence become separated. Keep subject and verb, parts of a verb phrase, and parts of commonly used paired concepts (like *if/then*) reasonably close together. If you don't, your reader has to spend so much time searching for the matching parts that the thread of the message is entirely lost.

Here is an example of the separation of subject and verb:

> If agencies are aware of the requirements of the Act, *the legal and administrative difficulties* which arise when contracts are drawn up, which do not specifically exclude government records from general arrangements to transfer government property or take some appropriate precautions in respect of them, *could be avoided.*

Here is an example of the separation of parts of the same verb:

> You *are*, within one month of receiving this notice, unless in the meantime you pay the arrears of rent in full and in cash, *required* to vacate the premises. In addition, you *must*, before vacating the premises, *arrange* for them to be cleaned thoroughly and *give* to the landlord all keys in your possession at the time.

The verbs concerned here are *are required, must arrange* and *must give* (*must* is doing double duty here in two verb phrases).

Here is an example of the separation of parts of a paired concept:

> *If* the purchaser of the land *does* not, within the period specified in the agreement, or such other documents such as extensions of time and other special considerations, *begin* building on the land in question, or at least start excavating for foundations, *then* the local authority may revoke the sale agreement....

It is a long way from the *if* section to the *then* section of this sentence. It is also a long way between parts of the verb *does begin.*

There are many ways of correcting these problems including shortening the sentences. However, one of the reasons sentences become long — through separation of subjects from their verbs — is that the writer has used passive instead of active verbs. We will look at this problem later in the chapter.

Exercise

Here are some long sentences. The first two illustrate the 'added-on' and the 'qualified' types. Look for the main ideas and break the sentences up so that the new sentences will contain only one main idea each.

1 It would be anticipated that, when the company takes over all of the complex, itself a significant item of local history, it would be possible to have, perhaps in association with a visitors' lounge, a display of significant locally produced artefacts and art of the district or indeed combine or co-locate the lounge and something which for want of a better term might loosely be called a museum.

2 The training section which is located on the fifth floor is open between 9 and 5 every weekday and anyone wanting to enrol in courses should come in person or phone Jane on extension 2345 because it will help you with your work and do a lot for your personal development which is important for you throughout your career.

3 (This sentence needs to be rearranged; use dot points (bullet points) to help make it easier to read).

In certain cases where a company employee is sued for damages, either alone or as co-defendant, or is prosecuted for an offence allegedly committed by him or her while in charge of a company vehicle in the course of his or her employment, the company may decide to arrange for his or her defence.

4 (This sentence is an extract from a lease. Try translating it bit by bit.)
If at the expiration of this Lease the Council shall have decided not to subdivide the said land and that it is not required for any authorised purpose and shall have declared the said land to be available for lease the Lessee shall be entitled to a further lease of the said land for such further term and at such rent and subject to such conditions as may then be provided by Statute Instrument or Regulation. [76 words]

Suggested solutions

1 The company will soon take over the complex which is of historical interest locally. We would like to have a visitors' lounge and a museum of local art and artefacts. It may be possible to combine these in one room.

2 The training section is on the fifth floor and is open between 9 and 5 every weekday. To enrol in courses, come in person or phone Jane on extension 2345. Doing appropriate courses will help you not only with your work but also with your personal development. It is important for you to develop personally throughout your career.

3 In certain cases, the company may decide to arrange for the defence of a company employee. This could happen when, for example
• he or she is sued for damages, either alone or as co-defendant;
• he or she is prosecuted for an offence allegedly committed while in charge of a company vehicle in the course of employment.

4 STEP 1: If at the expiration of this Lease
           If when this lease ends
the Council shall have decided
           the Council has decided
not to subdivide the said land
           not to subdivide the land
and that it is not required for any authorised purpose
           and that the Council does not need it
and shall have declared the said land to be available for lease
           and has declared the land to be available for lease
the Lessee shall be entitled to a further lease of the said land
           the Lessee may take up a further lease of the land
for such further term and at such rent and subject to such conditions
           for whatever term and rent and conditions
as may then be provided by Statute Instrument or Regulation
           as may then apply
STEP 2: If when this lease ends the Council has decided not to subdivide the land and that the Council does not need it and has declared the land to be available for lease, the Lessee may take up a further lease of the land for whatever term and rent and conditions as may then apply. [54 words]
STEP 3 (possible rewrite into separate shorter sentences): When this lease ends, the Council may have decided not to subdivide the land, and not to keep it for Council use. It may have declared the land to be available for lease. If so, the Lessee may take up a further lease of the land for whatever term, rent and conditions as may then apply. [22 + 11 + 23 = 56 words]

Note: This 'translation' clearly cuts a number of words from the clause. However, with legal documents, your next step must be to check that meaning has not been lost from the original. I have provided this suggested solution as an example of how sentence length can be controlled even in legal documents — you should not take it as an adequate replacement for the clause without consulting a lawyer.

Sentence length and readability

How long should a sentence be? That depends on your audience. If you are writing a magazine article, you could probably write about 20-22 words on average. Popular magazines are intended for leisure reading, so length of sentence is not vital. Check the average length of sentences in the magazines you are interested in. If you are writing technical and academic material, the average may be a little higher because you are writing for a narrow audience of people who understand your topic.

I am taking the view, in this book, that you are interested primarily in writing for the widest possible audience — the general public. This audience will not accept very long sentences, and the average sentence length should be about 12-15 words.

You should always consider the probable reading age of your audience. DSS forms are written for a reading age of 10–13 years. That means that you should write for an intelligent 10-year-old whenever you write anything intended for the general public. To write at a lower level is only acceptable when you are writing to an audience you know to be small children or people with reading problems. To write at a higher level is only acceptable when you are writing to an audience you know to have a tertiary education.

Assessing readability

You can assess the readability of sentences by using various tests. One of these is the Fog Index designed by Robert Gunning (*The Technique of Clear Writing* by Robert Gunning). It works like this:

1 Count the number of words in the passage you want to test.
2 Count the number of complete thoughts in the passage:
   - a simple or complex sentence is counted as one complete thought;
   - a compound sentence is counted as two thoughts if there are two independent clauses.
3 Work out the average sentence length:
   - divide the number of words in the passage by the number of complete thoughts.
4 Work out the percentage of 'hard words' — that is, words having three or more syllables:
   - not counting proper nouns; combinations of short, easy words; verb forms made into three syllables by adding *-ed* or *-es*;
   - work out percentage by dividing the number of hard words by the total number of words in the passage.
5 Add together the average sentence length (from 3) and the percentage of hard words (from 4).
6 Multiply the answer from step 5 by 0.4. This is the 'fog index'. (It is only an index — not words.)

Interpretation:

Index of 1-6   means the material is aimed at primary school level

Index of 7-12   means the material is aimed at secondary school level (general public)

Index of 13-16   means the material is aimed at university or college level

This and other similar devices should be taken with a grain of salt. The index is based on the premise that words having three or more syllables are 'hard'. We all know easy long words and hard short words. For example the word *hysterectomy* has as many as five syllables (hys-ter-ec-to-my) but we all know what it means; translating such a word into several shorter words would give a much longer sentence and a less precise meaning. A readability index should be used as a guide only. It is much more profitable to develop a sense of what is a good length of sentence for the audience you are writing for. You will only do this by practising writing and then testing yourself by getting others to read your efforts.

For practice, let us test the readability of the last few lines of the last paragraph, using the Gunning Fog Index.

A readability index should be used as a guide only. It is much more profitable to develop a sense of what is a good length of sentence for the audience you are writing for. You will only do this by practising writing and then testing yourself by getting others to read your efforts.

Number of words in the passage:	52
Number of complete thoughts:	4 (2 in last sentence)
Average sentence length:	13
Number of 'hard' words:	5 (*readability, profitable, develop, audience, practising*)
Percentage of 'hard' words:	9.6
Add 13 and 9.6:	22.6
Multiply 22.6 by 0.4:	<u>9.04</u>

The fog index is 9.04 which is well within the limits for general public reading.

Very short sentences

Writing too many short sentences one after the other in a document is almost as bad as writing too many long sentences. Certainly, short sentences are easy to understand. But very short sentences tend to follow a set grammatical pattern and to have a rhythm that you could almost beat on a drum. Look at this letter addressed to students:

Dear ....

Your assignments and examination papers have been marked. The marks are available from the secretary's office. Please collect all papers from the office by next Friday. If you do not, they will be held in the office until next term.

If you are re-enrolling, please see me before next Friday. Re-enrolment forms must be completed by then. Bring your identification number and a passport-size photo. These are needed for your new ID card.

There is nothing wrong grammatically with that letter. Also, each sentence is quite clear and the information has been divided logically between two paragraphs. So what's wrong with it? The sentences are so short and so much of a similar pattern that the reader is likely to switch off from sheer boredom. If you want people to read the whole of what you write, you first have to get their attention and next you have to keep it. This sort of 'machine-gun' writing, particularly in longer documents than this example, has a numbing effect on the reader. The constant repetition of the same pattern of stress and intonation in sentence after sentence makes everything dull — there is no highlighting.

Here is the pattern of the first sentences in that example. The first sentence is the model — by reading it aloud you can work out where the stress points fall (they are shown as high points on the line). The same pattern applies to all the sentences in the letter.

Your assignments and examination papers have been marked.

Three stress points marked with ∧
Final falling tone ╲

Let us re-write the letter using a mixture of long and short sentences and trying to vary their rhythmic patterns:

Dear ....

Your assignments and examination papers have been marked. You can get your marks from the secretary. Please collect all papers from the office by next Friday, or they will remain there until next term.

If you are re-enrolling, please see me before next Friday, which is the last day for completing the necessary forms. Bring your identification number and a passport-size photo, both of which are needed for your new ID card.

Of course, there are some occasions when very short sentences are the best kind to use. A few examples would be: instructions for evacuating a building, instructions for using a fire extinguisher, danger signs, road signs, instructions for taking medicine. Can you think of any more?

Arrangement within and between sentences

Earlier in this book, I suggested that a paragraph is only easy to read when it follows a logical pattern. I suggested that you start with the topic sentence, then write sentences that support the topic idea, and finish with a sentence that ties the paragraph together while giving a clue to the topic of the next paragraph.

This sort of organised writing should not be restricted to paragraphs. It should be apparent in sentences too. One important organisational point to remember is that people like to know what is going to happen in the order in which it is to happen. They like sentences to be written in chronological order.

So rather than writing

Your admission to the faculty will be processed as soon as you complete this form for which you will need to have with you a passport-size photo.

it would be better to write

> Please obtain a passport-size photo of yourself which you will need to attach to this form. Complete the form and return it to this office so that we may begin processing your admission to the faculty.

because the order of events is:

1 get the photo
2 attach it to the form
3 complete the whole form (and return it to the office)
4 processing

In this particular example I have added some information, writing it all as two sentences. We have already seen that 'shorter' is not necessarily 'better' from a plain English point of view. From time to time we will come across other examples of sentences that are improved by adding words.

Active and passive verbs

A great deal of bureaucratic writing is unclear because it uses passive verbs. Passive verbs make a sentence grammatically complete without necessarily showing the agent.

(Active)   *The manager* approved her leave application.
(Passive, with agent)   Her leave application was approved by *the manager*.
(Passive without agent)   Her leave application was approved.

People like to know who is responsible for things, and if you write sentences that do not have agents (doers of action), you do not show who is responsible for the action implied in the verb. People think that you don't care about them — that you think of them as just numbers and not as real people at all.

Put yourself in the shoes of the householder being addressed in this letter:

> Dear........
>
> In order that your application to vary your residential lease *may be processed,* it is necessary that the full name of the owner *be supplied*. The type of activity proposed should also *be described* on the attached form which *should be completed* and *returned* to the address shown. Near neighbours of the owner of the lease in question *will be questioned* to discover whether the proposed variation *is objected to*, and you *will be advised* when the situation *has been assessed*.

Who is the agent (doer) of each of the actions indicated by the italicised verbs? Whenever you see a passive verb in a sentence, you have to ask yourself .... *by whom?* Sometimes you can answer the question and sometimes you cannot. Can you in the example above?

> *may be processed* — by whom? presumably whoever sent the letter, that is, *us*
> *be supplied* — by whom? presumably the person addressed, that is, *you*
> *be described* — by *you*
> *should be completed* — by *you*

(should be) *returned* — by *you*
will be questioned — by *us*
is objected to — by *them* (thc ncighbours)
will be advised — by *us*
has been assessed — by *us*

To save the reader a lot of extra thinking about who is responsible for what, why not put at least some, if not all, of these verbs into the active voice? To do this, you have to turn the person responsible from the list above into the subjective form. For example, *us* becomes *we*, the subject of the first sentence:

Dear ....

In order that we may process your application to vary your residential lease, it is necessary that you supply your full name. You should also describe the type of activity proposed on the attached form which you should complete and return to the address shown. We will question your near neighbours to discover whether they object to the proposed variation, and we will advise you when we have assessed the situation.

Notice, too, that the rewritten passage is much shorter than the original. This is one more advantage of writing in active voice — the reader has less to read.

Some people feel that passive sentences are more 'objective' than active ones. This is nonsense. You can write just as objectively using active voice as you can using passive voice:

(Active) The members *felt* that she *would be* an inappropriate choice for delegate.
(Passive) She *was considered to be* an inappropriate choice for delegate.

Some sentences contain several passive verbs, each of which could have a different agent, if only we knew who it was:

The meeting to discuss applications for membership *was adjourned* at 5 pm because it *was agreed* that further information *should be obtained* before membership *could be granted* to two of the applicants.

By whom, in each case? Perhaps the doer of the action is the same in each case, but it may be different. The reader of the minutes has a right to know. Here is one solution:

At 5 pm *the chairman adjourned* the meeting to discuss applications for membership because *the meeting agreed* that *the secretary should obtain* further information before *council could grant* membership to two of the applicants.

It is not always wise to use active verbs. Sometimes we have to choose whether to write a sentence using active or passive verbs, depending on the meaning we want to give. In English, we tend to put into subject position in the sentence whatever we want to focus on. In the next two examples, subject position is first occupied by the doer of the action (active) and second by the receiver of the action (passive). When would we use each construction?

(1) *The teacher praised* the student for her good work.
(2) *The student was praised* by the teacher for her good work.

We would use (1) when the most important thing we want to say is that the *teacher* did a good thing, and we would use (2) when the most important thing we want to say is that the *student* did well.

Sometimes we cannot use active verbs at all, either because we don't know who the doer of the action is, or because it doesn't matter.

(1) While I was having breakfast in the hotel dining room, my room *was broken into* and my belongings *were tipped out* onto the floor.

(2) The low-lying parts of the town *were flooded* twice last year.

In (1), we have no idea who broke into the room or who tipped the belongings onto the floor. We could say *an intruder,* but how do we know whether there was only one intruder or several? In (2), it is not necessary to say what flooded the town — it is obvious.

In forms and in public information leaflets, you must write as concisely as possible.

People do not like reading forms, and they like filling them in even less, so the quicker and easier you can make the job the better. Active voice means shorter sentences than passive voice, so is ideal for the small space you can allow for instructions on a form. Decide which you prefer:

(Active)
Please answer all questions. Do not leave any blanks. If a question does not apply to you, write N/A in the space.

(Passive)
All questions should be answered. No blanks should be left. If a question is not applicable to you, N/A should be written in the space.

Leaflets should deal with one topic as briefly and understandably as possible — active voice allows you to use the imperative (command) mood of verbs where passive does not allow this so readily. Most people find the imperative mood is more direct, and therefore like it for instructions. Decide which you prefer:

(Active)
Prune* flowering cherry trees as soon as they *finish* flowering.

Don't burn fallen leaves; *rake* them up and *use* them as mulch in the garden.

*Prune is the imperative mood — the subject *you* is understood.

(Passive)
Flowering cherry trees *should be pruned* as soon as flowering *is finished.*

Fallen leaves *should* not *be burned;* they *should be raked* up and *used* as mulch in the garden.

You may be in the position of having to read, understand, and possibly rewrite, a document that someone else has written. If it is written largely in passive voice, you may have trouble reading it quickly. If someone else has to read it after you, or if you are editing it for publication, why not try to put as much as possible of it into active voice? Look at this sample:

(*Passive*)
It was announced yesterday by the Chairman that work on the City Hill project would be stopped until the current dispute could be settled. It had been decided that, if additional workers were to be hired so that the work could be completed on time, further disruption would be caused to other projects being undertaken by the company.

(*Attempted active*)
The Chairman announced yesterday that work on the City Hill project would stop until ___ could settle the current dispute. ___ had decided that if ___ were to hire additional workers in order to complete the work on time, they would cause further disruption to other projects that the company is undertaking.

The blanks indicate places where there should be an agent. However, it is impossible to put one in because there is no way of knowing, from the original passage, who the agent would be. For example, do we know exactly who will settle the current dispute? We don't, so we cannot use an active construction there. The solution is to write a mixture of active and passive, aiming to include more active than passive if possible.

(*Mixed active and passive solution*)
The Chairman announced yesterday that work on the City Hill project would stop until the current dispute could be settled. It* had been decided that if additional workers were to be hired in order to complete the work on time, they would cause further disruption to other projects that the company is undertaking.

* *It* is often used as a dummy subject. In the sentence *It is raining* there is no problem of understanding. In this sentence, however, the construction dodges owning up to who decided. You should try to find out who is responsible, and use the actual agent in subject position — for example, *A meeting of workers had decided...*

Exercise

Find the passive verbs in these passages and change them to active wherever practicable. You may have to supply an agent where one is not stated. Are there any sentences that should be left in passive form?

1 Your application is being considered by the board and the management team, and you will be advised when the chairman's final decision has been reached.
2 Reference is made to your conversation with Mr Gardner.
3 It has been decided to agree to this proposal.
4 His application for unemployment benefits has been turned down because it was discovered by departmental investigators that he had a

second job which had not been affected by the collapse of the building firm.

5 As a general principle, filling of vacancies on a part-time basis is to be discouraged. Any decision to fill a vacancy on a part-time basis is to be made personally by the Staff Manager.

6 It should be noted that ten places on the next course will be offered to members of your section. You will be notified as soon as plans have been completed, and you will then be required to see that your application is submitted as soon as possible.

7 After I was brought home by my friend, I discovered that my flat had been vandalised.

8 All the data was lost when the computer operator failed to save it.

9 The computer operator lost all the data when he failed to save it.

10 Your eligibility will be decided as soon as your application is lodged.

Suggested solutions

1 The board and the management team are considering your application, and we will advise you when the chairman has reached a final decision.

2 I refer to your conversation with Mr Gardner.

3 We have decided to agree to this proposal.

4 We have turned down his application for unemployment benefits because departmental investigators discovered that he had a second job which *had not been affected* by the collapse of the building firm. (There is hardly any point in changing the italicised passive verb to active in this sentence; the only possible agent, *collapse,* would make an awkward sentence.)

5 As a general principle, I discourage filling of vacancies on a part-time basis. The Staff Manager should decide personally whether to fill a vacancy on a part-time basis.

6 You should note that we will offer ten places on the next course to members of your section. We will notify you as soon as we have completed plans, and we will then require you to *submit* your application as soon as possible. (I have shortened *to see that you submit* to *submit* ; you may or may not agree with this; it makes the sentence shorter, but may alter the meaning.)

7 After my friend brought me home, I discovered that my flat *had been vandalised.* (We do not know who the agent is, so passive is the best construction.)

8 and 9 (You do not need to alter these sentences. Number 8 clearly implies that the loss of the data was more important than who caused the loss. Number 9 lays blame squarely on the computer operator.)

10 Lodge your application and we will then decide whether you are eligible. (Re-order this sentence to put it into chronological order.)

Verbs or verbal nouns?

Verbal nouns are nouns made by adding endings like -*ation*, -*ility*, -*ance* and -*ment* to verbs, or otherwise altering verbs to turn them into nouns. The practice is called, appropriately, **nominalisation**, itself an excellent example.

Verbal nouns seem to take all the life out of a sentence. Take this sentence, for instance — can you honestly visualise anybody actually doing anything?

> The workers will hold discussions about the project with whoever has the responsibility for its co-ordination.

It is lifeless. On the other hand, look at this sentence. It says the same thing, but uses verbs instead of verbal nouns to spell out the action.

The workers will *discuss* the project with whoever *is responsible* for *co-ordinating* it.

And action it is — in that sentence you could visualise people discussing, being responsible, and co-ordinating. Verbs are dynamic. Verbal nouns are static. Frequently (but not always), you can recognise a verbal noun by the article (the, a/an) or pronoun before it and the preposition after it:

The management of the firm was becoming more difficult.

This is easily altered to the verb form to make the whole sentence more lively:

Managing the firm was becoming more difficult.

Verbal nouns are not always so easy to spot. As you read a passage, ask yourself whether any of the longer nouns are derived from verbs. If they are, what are the verbs? Could you use a part of the verb instead of the verbal noun without losing meaning? If you could, do it.

Exercise
Find the verbal nouns in these passages. Then rewrite the passages using verb forms instead of verbal nouns wherever practicable. At the same time, try to eliminate unnecessary passive verbs, and make sentences shorter where you can.

1 There is an expectation that the performance of the duties of a position should be carried out by the substantive occupant; consideration will only be given to the occupation of a position by a temporary worker in exceptional circumstances.
2 The major aim of the study is to provide information which will assist the understanding of catchment behaviour and allow better management of the catchment as a whole and of this lake in particular. In the course of obtaining this information, it is hoped that a better understanding of the sedimentation rate within the lake, and the processes affecting it, will also be gained.
3 Would you please indicate your requirements for places on our next course?
4 There was a requirement for the Department to look ahead to the implementation of the new office structure in its development of a suitable training programme.

Suggested solutions

1 We expect that the substantive occupant will perform the duties of a position; we will only consider a temporary worker's occupying a position in exceptional circumstances.
2 The study will help us understand catchment behaviour so that we will better manage the catchment as a whole and this lake in particular. At the same time, we hope to learn more about the rate at which sediment forms in the lake and the processes involved.
3 How many places do you require on our next course?
4 The Department was required to look ahead to implementing the new office structure in developing a suitable training programme.

10 Choosing your words

When it is all boiled down, words are our basic tools. We use them for effect, and the effect they make depends on our selecting the right ones for the particular occasion. In this section we look at some aspects of the choice of words that are particularly relevant to plain English.

Pompous words

People who use long words often do so out of habit and with a desire to show off. They believe that using long words makes them appear more dignified, businesslike or official. The result is often just the opposite. Using long words when there are shorter words available that will do the job just as well shows their users to be pompous, indifferent to the reader and officious.

Sometimes a big word is just right for the purpose, provided that it is necessary for the topic, that the reader will understand it, and that you know how to use it. Take a word like *decentralisation*. It is certainly a long word, but if you are writing to somebody who knows what you are talking about, it makes sense to use it. How would you divide it up into little words, anyway? *Reversing a trend towards making things central* or *Moving smaller units away from the city* perhaps? If the meaning is clear from the context, you do not need to write in six words what you can write in one that the audience understands.

Mostly, however, people use big words to express small ideas, and that is silly. Why write *peruse* when *read* is there, why *domicile* or *residence* for *home*, *utilisation* for *use*? All you do when you use these unnecessarily big words is make the reader think harder than necessary. Remember, it is your job to be plain, not the reader's job to unravel your meaning.

You might say 'What's wrong with *residence*? It's a perfectly ordinary word'. So it is, but *home* is even more ordinary.

Or you might say 'Why should I lower my standards? People should widen their vocabularies. Why shouldn't they have to look up a word or two?'. You are not lowering your standards by using ordinary words — you are showing that you have done your homework and that you relate to your audience of ordinary people. You use ordinary words in speech — why change to anything else in writing? Yes, it's great if people can widen their vocabularies, but you are not their teacher — you are trying to tell them something. If you mask your message in a lesson in word-building, you fail as a communicator.

There are thousands of pompous words that could do with deflating to something more ordinary. Here are just a few of them. You should try to add to this list whenever you have the opportunity. Why not use the inside back cover of this book as a place to keep such lists?

Pompous	Plain
aggregation	total
approximately	about
ascertain	find out
assistance	aid, help
cognisant of	aware of
commendation	praise
customary channels	usual/regular way
deem	believe, consider
educational institution	school, college (specify)
effected, effectuated	made, did
endeavour, attempt	try
envisage	see, think
facilitate	help, make easy
functionalisation	use
implement	carry out, begin
initiate	begin
instantaneously	now
instrumentalities	means, ways
obtain	get
premises, dwelling, domicile	home, house, place
prior to	before
procedural practices	what to do and how to do it
pursuant to	under
requisition	order
subsequent to	after
terminate, determine (legal)	end
transpire	happen
viable	workable
yours, your communication	your letter, memo (specify)

Exercise

Translate these pompous sentences into ordinary sentences that would make better sense on first reading:

1 Consequent upon his confrontation with management, he was sent a copy of the regulations governing transportational procedures.
2 This is to acknowledge yours of 26 ult regarding your complaint pursuant to Section 9 of the byelaw which concerns prohibition of the utilisation of power lawnmowing devices prior to 7 am.

Suggested solutions

1 After his meeting with management, he was sent a copy of the rules for shipping goods.
2 Thank you for your letter of 26 (name of last month) setting out a complaint under Section 9 of the byelaw. This Section is about banning the use of power lawn mowers before 7 am.

Too many words

Redundancies

You only have to say something once. If you say it twice, you are not emphasising it — you are just confusing your reader. There are many expressions that contain the same idea said more than once. We use them both in speech and in writing. Why? Because sometimes we just don't know when to stop. Or because we need something to fill in time while we think of the next thing to say. They may be habitual, but we should *completely eliminate* them. (If something is *eliminated*, it is *completely gone*; there is no need to use both words.) Here are some more examples of redundancies:

each and every	first and foremost	various and sundry
and so on and so forth	component part	final outcome
fair, just and equitable	co-operate together	give, devise and bequeath
past memories	consensus of opinion	terrible tragedy
initial preparation	deeds and actions	that period of time
odd in appearance	of a cheap quality	field of psychology

Here is a sentence full of redundancies:

> First and foremost, I want to stress forcefully that we must co-operate together in our initial preparation in order to achieve a fair, just and equitable end result that will have meaningful relevance to each and every researcher in the field of psychology.

Cut out the redundancies, and we have a much shorter and more readable sentence:

> First, I want to stress that we must co-operate in our preparation in order to achieve a just result that will have relevance to every researcher in psychology.

Fillers

We often hedge when we can't think what to say next, or when we are getting ready to say something. We use these fillers as a way of clearing our throats. When we write, we should clear our throats silently — not let extra words appear on the page. They make our writing look as if we haven't done our homework — they are vague. Here are a few examples:

generally	practically	actually
kind of	certain	for all intents and purposes
various	basically	virtually

Here is an example:

> *For all intents and purposes,* there are *virtually* no wild animals left in *certain* areas of the park. *Practically* all the wildlife was destroyed by *various* means when humans invaded their home.

Learn to recognise fillers; they can simply be left out:

> There are no wild animals that we know of left in the north and west sectors of the park. Wildlife was destroyed when humans invaded their home and either shot them or deprived them of food.

Some words can leave room for misinterpretation because of their vagueness. They may even seem downright insulting to the reader:

Filler	Translation
it would seem that	I think so, but I really don't know for sure
it is generally agreed that	I haven't the faintest idea how many agree and how many don't
obviously	Can't you see?
as we can plainly see	Look, I'm pointing it out for you.
this is to inform you that	See — this is a piece of paper with a letter on it; letters contain information; therefore, I am informing you — now read on.

Here is an example which contains both fillers and redundancies:

Dear Mr Jones

I am writing to inform you that it would seem that there is a possibility that some staff have *anticipated in advance* the *ultimate outcome* of our negotiations. At the latest meeting, it was *generally* agreed that no decision could yet be made. *Obviously* there has been a misunderstanding.

Suggested rewrite:

Dear Mr Jones

It is possible that some staff have anticipated the outcome of our negotiations. At the latest meeting, a majority voted against making a decision yet. I am sorry there has been a misunderstanding.

Wordy phrases

There are many phrases that we use every day which could readily be compressed into one word. There is nothing wrong with the phrases, but anything that takes up more words than necessary gives the reader more to do. Remember, our task is to make the reader's job as easy as possible. Here are a few phrases, with suggestions for reducing them to one word. I am sure you can think of many more to add to your list:

the reason for due to the fact that in light of the fact that for the reason that due to	*because, why*
in the event that under circumstances in which	*if*
prior to in anticipation of	*before*
with reference to with regard to in reference to concerning the matter of	*about*
at this point in time	*now*
is able to	*can*

Here is an example:

Thank you for your letter *concerning the matter of* your new home. *We are, at this point in time, not in a position* to offer you anything suitable *in light of the fact that* we have no 5-bedroom houses available.

Let's get to the point:

Thank you for your letter about your new home. We cannot offer you anything suitable because we do not have any 5-bedroom houses available.

Too many nouns

In an effort to write concisely, some writers try to cram too much information into a small number of words, usually nouns or a combination of nouns and adjectives. Unfortunately, this can cause problems because too many ideas are combined and the logical order of the ideas has to be reversed. As a result the reader has to unscramble an unwieldy string of words by working through it several times. Look at this example:

Inadequate staff performance review opportunities have led to staff dissatisfaction during the year.

Faced with such a collection of words, the reader stumbles and loses the thread of the document. We can cope with only a small number of units of information at once. This sentence asks the reader first to understand the individual words in the italicised phrase, second to understand what it means (this involves working backwards through the words), and finally to understand the phrase as the subject of the sentence. This is far too much work to give a reader to do. Most of us can manage two or three nouns in a string, but a string of four nouns and an adjective is too difficult.

How, in fact, do we understand such a string of words? The trick is to go to the end of the string and work backwards, using prepositions between the words to help with the unravelling:

Inadequate staff performance review opportunities
     1   5   4   3   2

= Inadequate opportunities (to) review performance (of) staff
     1   2   3   4   5

Plain English is not necessarily always shorter than English which is not plain. Sometimes it is better to use a few more words in order to be quite clear.

Overworked expressions — clichés

Many words, phrases, clauses and whole sentences that business people use have been worked to death. If we continue to use them, we give the impression that we cannot think for ourselves. Most of these expressions were somewhere near to everyday speech when they were first used, but nobody uses them in everyday conversation nowadays. We have just copied them from other people's writing. We should stop the copying habit right here by avoiding expressions such as these:

after giving due consideration

at this time we wish to state

at your earliest convenience

in accordance with your request

your kind and esteemed favour

please find enclosed

please be advised that

Some, that begin with the present participle of a verb (the *-ing* part), must never be used to take the place of whole sentences, and should be avoided entirely:

assuring you of our cooperation

assuring you of our best attention at all times

thanking you in advance

referring to yours of recent/even date

There are many more such expressions. Watch for them in the mail that you receive, and resolve never to use any of them yourself.

Overuse of 'you'

Later we will discuss the advantages of using *you* and *me* in working documents to create a personal approach. However, in this section, let us look at a use of *you* which causes wordiness.

Look at this sentence:

You should have seen the mess my desk was in.

Who is meant by *you*? Is it the reader personally? Is it 'everyone'? No, it's neither. In fact, *you* is quite meaningless here, and the sentence would be tighter if all reference to *you* could be left out.

My desk was in a mess.

Try to avoid this meaningless use of *you* which only contributes to wordiness. If you write such a sentence, rewrite it eliminating the *you* — the sentence will be simpler as a result.

Using buzz words

Buzz words are words used in the jargon of particular subjects, eg 'flexi' study and 'open learning' are buzz words used to describe a system of learning in which the student negotiates a flexible timetable of work, to study and to meet tutors at mutually convenient times. 'Incentive holidays' is a buzz phrase used in the travel industry, when an organisation provides a holiday as a reward to its most successful employees. Buzz words are useful, but usually only within the limits of particular subjects. If used outside those limits, they generally become meaningless.

Exercise

Get rid of all examples of wordiness in these sentences:

1 There is not a high degree of certainty about prospects for possible future employment opportunities facing those people engaged in undertaking studies at the graduate level in schools of higher learning in the future that lies ahead of them.

2 Dear Sir: Pursuant to your recent request for information and in reference to yours of even date, contents duly noted, please be advised that at this time we wish to state that, after giving the matter due consideration, we are unable to accede to your request.

3 If we try to anticipate in advance what is likely to happen to completely eliminate present household chores that we have to do today, we are likely to make mistakes because past history tells us that we are always unexpectedly surprised by the eventual outcome of events.

4 The organisations that provide aid and assistance to people who take part in the program activities we have arranged have returned back to the original methods that they employed earlier.

5 In the event that it rains later today, we will still have our picnic despite the fact that the majority of the class forgot to bring raincoats.

6 If you want to prevent air pollution, you should take your car to the service station for a tune-up twice a year.

Suggested solutions

1 Graduate students face uncertainty of employment opportunities in the future.
2 Dear Sir: Thank you for your letters of (dates). I am sorry that we cannot grant your request now as our stocks are being replaced. When we receive fresh stocks, I will send you the material you need.
3 If we try to anticipate what is likely to happen to eliminate present household chores, we are likely to make mistakes because history tells us that we are always surprised by the outcome of events.
4 The organisations that help people in our programs have reverted to their earlier methods.
5 If it rains later today, we will still have our picnic although most of the class forgot to bring raincoats.
6 To prevent air pollution, take your car to the service station for a tune-up twice a year.

Writing positively

Negative words indicate negative attitude. People think positively, and if you write something negatively that could just as easily have been written positively, you give the reader a negative opinion of you. For example, why write

It is *not possible* for us to send you the goods you ordered as *you failed* to enclose a cheque.

when it is just as easy to write this?

As soon as your cheque reaches us, we will be happy to fill your order.

You may have noticed that signs about smoking in public places and offices have changed in recent years. Signs used to read **No Smoking**. Nowadays, most signs read **Thank you for not smoking** or **This is a smoke-free area.** The old sign was clearly negative in attitude, whereas the modern signs try to get the reader on side by being as positive as possible.

Foreign words

English is a rich, living language. As such, it has an enormous variety of words to choose from. You should have no difficulty choosing just the right word to get your meaning across. There is no need to borrow words from other languages. Using Latin or French words does not show how educated you are — it just shows that you have not considered your audience. Some foreign expressions are used so blindly by people who have no idea what they mean that it is essential to include this warning here.

Re is not short for *regarding*. It is one form of the Latin word *res* and people who use it are saying to the reader 'about the thing' or 'about the matter' and then proceeding to say what the subject is. It is better to write the subject alone without any announcement that it is a subject. (Incidentally, *in re* is even worse; it says 'in about the thing', which is not grammatically correct either in Latin or in English.)

Per is Latin for *through* or *by means of*. It is nonsense, therefore, to write *per contract* and *as per*. Even such common expressions as *per hour, per diem* and *per annum* are more understandable if they are written in English as *an hour, a day* and *a year* respectively.

Idioms

Some groups of words cannot be explained by grammar — we just know that they are right in our language. Such groups are called idioms. They are established in the language by usage, and even slight variations can change the meaning entirely. Usually, it is variation in a following preposition that makes all the difference.

For example, you can *agree **with*** a person, *agree **to*** sell your car or *agree **on*** a price; you *agree **between*** the two of you and *agree **among*** the whole group; you *agree **on*** selling, but you *agree **to*** sell. If you don't like the entire deal, you can *agree **in*** part. You are *responsible **to*** your boss and *responsible **for*** getting a job done. You might live *adjacent **to*** a school, be *capable **of*** winning, have a *capacity **for*** doing better, find figures *identical **with*** mine, *differ **with*** me and come to a conclusion *different **from*** mine. You can be a *teacher* **of**, **at**, **in** or **for** depending on what follows.

Variation in word order also makes a difference to meaning. Contrast these two sentences:

I can see *through* your plan.

I can see your plan *through*.

Exercise

Insert the appropriate preposition in the blanks provided:

1 The block of flats is adjacent _____ the main street.
2 The old woman was afflicted _____ arthritis.
3 She is responsible _____ her employer _____ the training _____ junior staff.

4 I confide _____ my grandmother.
5 He has an aptitude _____ accounting which he is learning at college.
6 Uncaring people are indifferent _____ the sufferings of the poor.
7 He is an adviser _____ mathematics.
He is an adviser _____ the university.
He is an adviser _____ first-year students.
He is an adviser _____ this term only.

Solutions

1 to; 2 with; 3 to, for, of; 4 in; 5 for; 6 to; 7 in, at, of, for

Technical terms

Every occupation has its technical language, called **jargon**, which is superimposed on ordinary English. If you are a doctor, you understand *prognosis,* *appendectomy* and *subdural haematoma.* If you are a soldier, you understand *nocturnal bivouacs.* If you are a soil conservationist, *cores of sediment* bear no relation to apple cores except in shape.

If you are writing to an audience that understands your jargon, and if you are sure that nobody else is likely to have to read your document, by all means use jargon. It doesn't matter if outsiders cannot understand it. But this is the exceptional situation. Mostly, you are writing for a wider audience than just the people in your field. Would you understand this note from your doctor?

> Johnny has a *subdural haematoma* from a blow to the head, and the severe pain in his side warrants an immediate *appendectomy.* The *prognosis* is good, provided we operate quickly. Please come to the hospital to sign the necessary consent forms.

Perhaps you could work it out by delving into a good dictionary, but it seems to be urgent, and you cannot be bothered with having to look up obscure words when you are worried. It would have been just as easy for the doctor to write

> He has some bruising and internal bleeding from a blow to the head, and the severe pain in his side warrants an immediate operation to remove his appendix. The outlook is good, provided we operate quickly. Please come to the hospital to sign the necessary consent forms.

The golden rule about using jargon is: When in doubt, don't. However, there are occasions when a technical term is the best term available — the only one that really says what you want to say. In that case, use it but explain it. There are several ways of explaining a technical term:

1 *Include it in a glossary at the beginning or end of the document:* A glossary is a kind of dictionary in which you give terms which could have different meanings in different contexts. You give the term, plus the meaning which applies in your context only. The reader cannot then blame you if he or she misunderstands the term.

For example, in a paper on kinship written by an anthropologist, the following entry might appear in a glossary of terms:

COLLATERAL — the siblings of lineal relatives (parents, grandparents) and their descendants

which is a far cry from the financial meaning of *collateral*.

2 *Give a definition on the spot*: Either interrupt the sentence and put your explanation in brackets, or give a definition in a separate sentence immediately afterwards.

For example, an introductory textbook on linguistics should explain new terms the first time they are mentioned. It could be written:

.... Chapter 2 is about *phonetics* (the analysis of speech sounds with respect to their articulation, acoustic properties and perception) and Chapter 3 is about ..

or

... Chapter 2 is about *phonetics*. Phonetics is the analysis of speech sounds with respect to their articulation, acoustic properties and perception. Chapter 3 is about ...

This is a good example, too, of what you do not have to explain. Notice that the author has not explained *articulation, acoustic* and *perception*. These terms would be explained in the appropriate place — in the chapter on phonetics.

3 *Tell a story:* Sometimes it is not feasible to give a definition. It may be better to show how a difficult concept works in practice. Several good examples of this method of explanation are included in leaflet V100 Registering and Licensing your motor vehicle — some notes to help you, available at main post offices.

Some insurance companies are writing their policies in plain English now, but, while the words and sentences are straightforward, they are still stuck with ideas that are hard to get across to ordinary people. Here is how one difficult concept could be explained by telling a story:

We have designed this policy to give you and your family extra liability protection above and beyond the coverage of your present motor vehicle, household and other policies.......

Suppose you have a standard motor vehicle policy that covers you up to a £300 000 liability limit for bodily injury for each accident. With our policy you are covered even if a court says you have to pay £1 300 000.......
(This is an imaginary document.)

Using personal pronouns

Do you have difficulty using personal pronouns in your writing? That is, do you find it hard to write a sentence like this?

We have had to reject your application because you did not submit it to us in time for us to include it in this year's allocation of funds.

If you do, you are not alone. Many people find it difficult to use personal pronouns like this, and prefer to hide behind their organisations:

Application No 1234 has been rejected by this Department because submission was not effected in time for inclusion in this year's allocation of funds.

Do you see what has happened? Not only have all the personal pronouns disappeared, but the whole thing has been twisted into passive voice, and is full of verbal nouns too. It is now an entirely lifeless piece of writing. The reader would be forgiven for thinking that a block of concrete wrote it. If you want you and your Department or company to be regarded as real people who care about other real people, you will have to try to use personal pronouns occasionally. It is not always possible, but use them where you can. You will get a much better response from your public if you do.

Imagine that someone came to the front counter of your office and said to your receptionist: 'Good morning. Here is my application for a grant.' Your receptionist would not say: 'Good morning. This application is too late. It should have been submitted by yesterday for inclusion in this year's allocation of funds. As it is, the best advice of this Department is for the application to be kept until next year and a note made of next year's closing date.' That sounds as if it has been learned. It is unfriendly. The receptionist would probably say instead: 'Good morning. I am sorry, this application is too late. You should have submitted it by yesterday so that we could include it in this year's allocation of funds. As it is, I suggest you keep it and make a note of next year's closing date. Better luck next time.'

The way to write a letter so that it has the same force as spoken language is to address your reader as a person, by using *you* for the person you are addressing and *I* or *we* for yourself or your organisation. This practice has the bonus that sentences are written in active voice and without too many verbal nouns. You would seem to be taking more of an interest in whoever is going to be reading your letter if you say:

> *We* have had to reject *your* application because *you* did not submit it to *us* in time for *us* to include it in this year's allocation of funds.

Contractions

It is not a good idea to use contractions of words when you are writing. So write *cannot* and *do not* rather than *can't* and *don't*. People do not like reading contractions in letters, reports and other business documents. One reason is that they consider contractions to be too much part of colloquial expression, and so they believe that they do not have a place in more formal business writing. Another possible reason is that many people have trouble spelling those contractions themselves — for example *couldn't* is frequently spelled wrongly as *could'nt*. Faced with the correct spelling, a reader may pause and wonder about the spelling. Any pause in reading means that the reader has lost the thread of the sentence and has to start again. Your aim as a writer is to do everything possible to make the reading process painless, so avoid the problem by spelling these words and phrases out fully.

Variation for variation's sake

Another way to lose a reader is to provide him or her with too many words for the same idea in a short document. Look at this example from an advertisement:

Your *children's* shoes are important. *Kids'* feet need room to grow, so cramming them into footwear that is too tight only causes the *youngsters* to develop badly. The feet of the *youth* of Britain deserve the best. Buy ...

In a short document like this, it is ridiculous to use four different words to refer to the same thing. While it might be slightly more acceptable in advertising than in business correspondence, many people believe they have to vary the words dealing with their main theme. The practice merely causes the reader to stop with a jerk at every change of word to make sure that he or she is still reading about the same thing. There may be some excuse for variety of expression in a long document, but in something as short as a letter or a public information leaflet, consistency of expression is more important to the reader.

Exercise

Now that we have covered the important aspects of the mechanics of writing in plain English, you should be able to edit gobbledegook, as unclear English is generally known. Rewrite this letter in plain English:

Dear Mr Green

Receipt is acknowledged of yours of 18 inst regarding remuneration for services rendered by this organisation in re the removal of building materials surplus to requirement from your residential address.

As was so kindly observed by you in your communication, the charge for the removal of the said material is somewhat less than the amount previously quoted by us beforehand. This, you can be assured, is not due to any error in our accounting department, as you suggested, but rather is due to the fact that, since speaking to you on the telephone where we gave our quote for the aforementioned removal job, we have been able to streamline our work practices to the extent that they are now so efficient that we are actually saving money. The final outcome of all this is that the savings have been able to be passed on to our customers.

We apologise if the new price schedule which was sent to you didn't reach you because we did send this list to everyone several weeks ago, but anyway please find enclosed another copy for your information.

Hoping to be of continuing service to you in the future.

Yours sincerely

Suggested solutions

(you may have other suggestions — be prepared to back them up)

Dear Mr Green

Thank you for your letter of 18 (this month) about payment for removing surplus building materials from your home.

The charge is less than we quoted because we have recently streamlined our work practices and are now saving money. We have passed these savings on to our customers.

A copy of our new price schedule is enclosed.

Yours sincerely

Explanations:

Paragraph 1

Receipt is acknowledged is archaic and passive and therefore unfriendly.
yours is not specific.
inst, prox and *ult* are abbreviations of Latin words meaning this month, next month and last month respectively — better to use English and name the month.
for services rendered can be omitted because the actual services are specified in the next line.
in re is Latin — use English (it can be omitted here anyway).
the removal of — verbal noun: better to use the verb form *removing*.
surplus to requirement and *residential address* are wordy.

Paragraph 2

Note the bracketed sections. They include redundancies and other wordiness, negativity (better to tell the reader something positive) and unnecessarily telling the reader what he told you. Try reading just the remaining *italic* sections. When these are tidied up for grammar and plain English, the paragraph is much smoother.

[As was so kindly observed by you in your communication,] *the charge* [for the removal of the said material] *is* [somewhat] *less than* [the amount previously] *quoted* [by us beforehand.] *This,* [you can be assured, is not due to any error in our accounting department, as you suggested, but rather] *is due to the fact that, since* [speaking to you on the telephone where] *we gave our quote* [for the aforementioned removal job], *we have been able to streamline our work practices* [to the extent that they are now] *so* [efficient] *that we are* [actually] *saving money.* [The final outcome of all this is that] *the savings have been able to be passed on to our customers.*

Paragraphs 3 and 4

price schedule / list — stick to one term for this item.
didn't — better to use *did not* (avoid contractions).
please find enclosed — archaic expression: prefer *I am enclosing* OR *Enclosed is.*
for your information — omit this because it is obvious.
Hoping.... — fragment: always use whole sentences.
continuing and *in the future* express the same thought — redundancy.

Revision exercise

This exercise can be used as a revision. There are 25 sentences, each one with at least one major structural error in it. Identify the error and then rewrite the sentence correctly. Try doing five sentences at a time.

1 After a while, she began to enjoy her job. An enjoyment shared by those who like to see a task well done.
2 There is good news today for the department, tomorrow it moves to its new building.
3 I read where the Prime Minister made a speech on the subject in Glasgow.
4 He said that the reason why he had stopped running in the Fun Run was because he was tired.
5 Shane Gould was one of the best swimmers Australia has ever produced, and she lives quietly on a farm with her husband and children.
6 The dishes are washed up and the house clean.
7 The secretary and treasurer of the tennis club were both present at the meeting.
8 We did better than expected this year: we were even winners in our match against Cardiff.
9 This sample bottle of perfume comes to you with our compliments which we hope you will find pleasant.
10 The floor manager asked the studio audience to vigorously clap when he waved his arms in the air.
11 Opening the window, the scent of jasmine on the night air struck her as overpowering.
12 When she was six years old, her grandmother died and left her a small legacy.
13 They haven't scarcely any resources worth mentioning about.
14 I liked her more than Kate.
15 He may apply for a job as a clerical assistant, a salesman, or cooking in the army.
16 Those people lying down over there are either lazy or they don't feel well.
17 There was one thing I enjoyed more than anything else about my course. It is the good friends I made while I was at college.
18 All the elderly residents of the home were rescued by the brave firefighters, and the building was a total write-off.
19 After receiving first aid for his injured ankle, the ambulance officers rushed him to hospital for X-rays.
20 I asked you to remind me to show you the photo I took of the dog when you visited us.
21 The lecturer advised the students to be punctual, that they should do all assignments, and she said they should attend all tutorials.
22 On examining the goods, they were found to be faulty.
23 The purpose of the meeting is to elect office bearers for the coming year and a welcoming barbecue for new members.
24 My sister is a governor on the local school board. One of three women elected this year.
25 There was a huge crash and then the lights go out.

Explanations and suggested solutions

1 The words after the full stop do not constitute a complete sentence — they form only a *fragment*. Provide a complete subject and verb:
    After a while, she began to enjoy her job. This kind of enjoyment is shared by those who like to see a task well done.

2 This is the *comma fault* — using a comma when a semi-colon would be better to indicate that a new, but related, thought is beginning.
    There is good news today for the department; tomorrow it moves to its new building.

3 Do not use an *adverbial clause as a noun clause*. The noun clause should begin with *that* and not with *where*.
    I read that the Prime Minister made a speech on the subject in Glasgow.

4 The same idea is expressed three ways — this is called *redundancy* or *tautology*. The words *reason*, *why* and *because* all express the same idea — remove two of them:
    He said that he had stopped running in the Fun Run because he was tired.

5 This sentence combines two *unrelated ideas*. The fact that Shane Gould was a good swimmer has nothing to do with the fact that she lives on a farm. The two ideas should be separated into two sentences:
    Shane Gould was one of the best swimmers Australia has ever produced. She lives quietly on a farm with her husband and children.

6 An *essential verb* has been omitted. When the subjects in a compound sentence are different in number, their verbs must also be different in number to match:
    The dishes are washed up and the house is clean.

7 This construction implies that the jobs of secretary and treasurer are being done by the same person. If you mean that two people are involved, put the article *the* before each of them:
    The secretary and the treasurer of the tennis club were both present at the meeting.

8 The adverb *even* is misplaced. It is easy to misplace adverbs like *even, just* and *only* By doing so, you alter the meaning of the sentence. This sentence implies surprise at our being winners — it should imply that we did well against all competition, even against the strong Cardiff team:
    We did better than expected this year: we were winners even in our match against Cardiff.

9 *Which* does not refer back accurately. We expect *which* and *that* to refer back to the noun or noun phrase immediately before it, but this sentence is ambiguous — it seems as if either the compliments or the perfume could be what you find pleasant. Perhaps so! However, sentences should not be capable of more than one reading. If you mean *which* to refer to the perfume, write the sentence like this:
    This sample bottle of perfume, which we hope you will find pleasant, comes to you with our compliments.

10 Do not *split infinitives*, or indeed any other verb phrases, without good reason:
    The floor manager asked the studio audience to clap vigorously when he waved his arms in the air.

11 Opening the window is a *dangling modifier* — it has nothing in the sentence to modify. *The scent* did not open the window — *'she'* did:
    Opening the window, she was overpowered by the scent of jasmine on the night air.

12 *Ambiguity* is caused here by the omission of a complete subject — the pronoun *she* could refer to either the grandmother or the child. To avoid ambiguity, restore the noun phrase:
    When the child was six years old, her grandmother died and left her a small legacy.

13 *Double negatives* are sometimes used in colloquial speech for emphasis. They are not used in formal English. Do not write *not hardly, not scarcely, not never*, or similar double negatives.
    Likewise, there are some verbs which do not need a following preposition because the idea is already contained in the verb. One of these is *comprise* — we do not write

comprising of because *comprising* means *consisting of*. *Mentioning* means *talking about,* so to write *mentioning about* is redundant.
They have scarcely any resources worth mentioning.

14 It is not clear in this sentence whether I liked her more than Kate liked her or I liked her better than I liked Kate. We should avoid all forms of *ambiguity* and write precisely what we mean — here are both solutions:
I liked her more than Kate did.
I liked her better than I liked Kate.

15 This sentence *lacks parallel construction*. It is easier for a reader to follow a sentence if we stick to the structure we begin with:
He may apply for a job as a clerical assistant, a salesman, or an army cook.

16 This sentence also *lacks parallel construction*. When you use connecting pairs such as *either...or,* each part of the pair must be followed by the same construction:
Those people lying down over there are either lazy or unwell.

17 *Do not switch the tense of verbs* unnecessarily. If you begin talking about something that occurred in the past, use the past tense throughout the story.
There was one thing I enjoyed more than anything else about my course. It was the good friends I made while I was at college.

18 The co-ordinating conjunction *and* is used to join *like things*. When you want to show *contrast,* use *but* :
All the elderly residents of the home were rescued by the brave firefighters, but the building was a total write-off.

19 *Dangling modifier* again: at first sight, the reader gets the impression that the ambulance officers injured their ankles. It is only when you read more carefully that you realise that something is wrong. Make sure that a modifier has something to modify:
After giving him first aid for his injured ankle, the ambulance officers rushed him to hospital for X-rays.

20 This sentence does not make clear what the words *when you visited us* relate to. The fault lies with *when*. It would be better to use more specific wording and word order. There are two solutions:
I asked you to remind me, the next time you visited us, to show you the photo I took of the dog.
I asked you to remind me to show you the photo of the dog that I took the last time you visited us.

21 *Parallel construction* again: in this sentence, three quite different constructions have been used. The reader has to mentally readjust to each new construction while reading, and this slows reading and makes it less smooth than it should be. Stick to one construction only — here is one of the three possible solutions:
The lecturer advised the students to be punctual, to do all assignments and to attend all tutorials.

22 *Dangling modifier* again: in this sentence, we are not told who examined the goods. Part of the problem is that the sentence is in the *passive* voice — a rewrite in active voice would be better:
When we examined the goods, we found that they were faulty.

23 *Parallel structure* again: in this sentence, the writer has switched from a verb structure to a noun structure. Here is one solution:
The purpose of the meeting is to elect office bearers for the coming year and to welcome new members at a barbecue.

24 The second part is a *fragment*. Here is a solution which combines the two parts into one sentence:
My sister, who is a governor on the local school board, is one of three women elected this year.

25 *Do not switch the tense* of verbs when the time should be the same — if something happened in the past, use the past tense when describing it:
There was a huge crash and then the lights went out.

11 Principles of effective writing and document design

Any document you write is a messenger of everything about you and what you intend to say. It will only work if it observes the principles of effective writing and the principles of *good document design*.

So far, we have discussed grammatically correct English. We have also discussed the aspects of writing which can make grammatically correct English easy to read. But there is more to writing than the mechanics of it. If you want to be fully involved with your writing, you need to know why you are writing in the ways I have suggested you should. This means looking more closely at the principles of writing. We will also look at how design relates to them, and how you can use design to enhance the impression your documents make

The principles of effective writing

The points you need to bear in mind in relation to everything you write are:

- the Topic
- the Purpose
- the Context
- the Audience
- the Language
- and the Package

Topic

The topic of a document is what it is all about. Decide what the topic is and stick to it. It is very tempting to try to cram two or more topics in the one document, but this only makes the reader annoyed. You are asking the reader to switch thought patterns abruptly if you include more than one main topic in a document. Readers like to read all you want to say about one topic, allowing you to lead them through it and helping them to arrive at conclusions. If you give them two topics to absorb, neither will get full attention, and misunderstandings can result in the ensuing mix-up of thinking. If you have to write about two distinctly different topics, write two separate documents. Of course, there are bound to be sub-topics within any document — in a report, for instance, you may have to report on three or four aspects of the matter; but in this case they are all related and are necessary for the report to be complete.

There is one question you should ask yourself before you go any further: Do I have to write about this topic at all? If you can deal with it by means of a telephone call or by visiting an office along the corridor, or if there is no need for a written record for the file, don't write anything. There is already too much paper circulating around offices — why add to it if you don't need to?

Purpose

There are two main purposes in all business and administrative writing — to give information and to get information.

If your purpose is to give information, be precise, give the complete story so that there can be no doubt in the reader's mind about what you mean, and make sure that your facts are accurate.

If your purpose is to get information, ask specific questions and make sure that the reader understands why you need the information.

Context

People see documents in the context of their relevance to them personally and to their organisations. If a document does not seem relevant to them, they will not read it as closely as you might like them to.

Is your document one of a series, or a one-off document? If it is one of a series, how does it fit with the others in the series? If it is early in the series, you cannot assume that readers will understand too many technical terms, so you must explain them. Later in the series, you can assume that readers have read the earlier documents.

How will your readers relate personally to your document? For example, if in writing a sales brochure you use the language of a formal report, you will not sell your product. Consider what kind of language is expected of you in the circumstances.

Consider also how to make the topic interesting. Is it one that readers will automatically want to know about? In many cases they may not see how it affects them. Is it one that they should be interested in for their own safety? If readers can see that something is important to them personally, they are more likely to read it.

Audience

The people you write to constitute the most important element in effective writing. If you write without knowing anything about your audience, you deserve to have your writing consigned to the rubbish bin.

You should know whether you are writing for one person or a group, for a colleague or a total stranger, for a homogeneous group (for example, all one sex, similar age groups, same profession), or for the general public.Your writing should be different in each case. If you are writing for a colleague, you can afford to use some technical terms that you could not use in correspondence with a stranger. If you are writing for children, you know you must keep your language simple and perhaps include pictures. If you are writing for the general public (the most common audience) you must write for people whose average reading age is reckoned to be about 11 years, and not for people who would need a PhD to understand your message.

There are many things you should ask about the audience in addition to who they are. You need to know what they already know about the topic, so that you know at what level you can start writing. You need to know what the audience has to be told — maybe you need to tell them how to vote at the next general election; you cannot assume that they will remember from last time, or even that they voted last time.

You cannot put yourself into the shoes of your audience satisfactorily by imagination alone. You will need help to find out all this about your audience. It may mean that you will need to talk to someone else , or go out into the streets and conduct a survey; or you may have to invite representative groups into your office and use them to sound out ideas for your document.

People will react best to your writing if you keep in mind that you are writing to individuals, not objects; that way you will force yourself to write the sort of prose which represents the way you would speak to them if you could talk to them face-to-face.

Language

This book is almost entirely about language. It is about the mechanics of language — what works and what does not work. You know by now that you should check your writing for grammatical correctness. It is also your job to make your message plain enough to be understood by your audience at first reading, and that means writing in plain English. Additionally you need to think about the language in general. Within the bounds of grammatical correctness and of plain English there are many choices available. Think about those choices. You need to be familiar with a wide range of commonly-used words so that you can choose from them those which suit the topic you are writing about and the audience you are writing for.

Package

The final aspect that we need to consider, and the one that we will consider in the most detail here, is the design or packaging of the document. Many people are not concerned with anything more than just the words a document contains. However, if you are to be a truly effective writer, you have to consider more than just the words — you have to consider the presentation of the document. By the same token, if you are to be a truly effective forms designer, for instance, you have to consider more than just the layout — you have to consider the words of the questions on the form and what they mean to the form-filler and the form-processor.

As most workplaces these days are equipped with computers, word processors and electronic typewriters, we will be looking at some of the things we can do with these machines to make our work more presentable.

Many people are now moving away from specialised jobs to ones where several skills can be used. Keyboarders are learning to write their own documents; clerical workers are learning keyboarding; everyone is learning filing. Workers are moving from skill to skill in the course of a day, and no skill is the exclusive preserve of any one group of people. The outcome of this office revolution is that many more people than before are being made responsible for whole documents; they are being asked to plan, write, design and do keyboarding. You may find that you have to take a document through the whole publication process. That means knowing what you are talking about when you talk to the people who do part of the job for you so that the job turns out the way you want it.

White space
Often, the most obvious thing about a bad document is that it lacks white space.

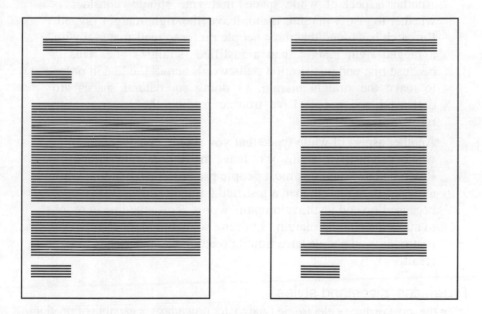

The letter on the left is crammed on the page. The left and right margins are too narrow and the paragraphs seem to be too long. It gives a bad impression because there seems to be too much to comprehend in one reading. It doesn't matter that the English may be perfect and as plain as possible. It is a loser because of its crowded appearance.

The letter on the right, on the other hand, gives a good first impression and therefore stands a much better chance of being read straight away than the one on the left. The margins are much wider, the material seems to have been divided up into shorter paragraphs, and one paragraph has been inset in order to highlight it. Whether the English is readable or not, the impression this letter gives makes it the winner on looks.

First impressions are very important, and you should try to give your writing the best possible chance of getting its message across by presenting it attractively. Of course, if the language does not match the presentation, the document will lose anyway; but if the total package is good, the message will get through.

A letter like the one on the left should be spread to a second page rather than crammed on one page.

Another aspect of white space that you should consider is whether to justify (straighten) margins or to leave the right margin ragged. Research has found that most people prefer to read material with a ragged right margin than a justified one. This is because line-end justification pulls words across the line in order to make the straight margin. In doing so, natural spaces are destroyed, and people have trouble reading the material as a result. Ragged right margin preserves the natural spaces between words. Here is part of this paragraph again — first with a justified right margin and then with a ragged right margin. Decide which you prefer. Test how long it takes to read them:

> Another aspect of white space that you should consider is whether to justify margins or to leave the right margin ragged. Research has found that most people prefer to read material with a ragged right margin than a justified (straight) one. This is because line-end justification pulls words across the line in order to make the straight margin. In doing so, natural spaces are destroyed, and people have trouble reading the material as a result.

> Another aspect of white space that you should consider is whether to justify margins or to leave the right margin ragged. Research has found that most people prefer to read material with a ragged right margin than a justified (straight) one. This is because line-end justification pulls words across the line in order to make the straight margin. In doing so, natural spaces are destroyed, and people have trouble reading the material as a result.

Typefaces, sizes and styles

Even the most ordinary electronic typewriter nowadays is capable of producing at least plain and bold versions of one typeface, probably also italic style, and several sizes. To illustrate, here is part of the enormous variety that can be achieved with just one typeface on one computer:

9 point lower case and UPPER CASE Helvetica plain and <u>underscored</u>

9 point lower case and UPPER CASE Helvetica bold and <u>underscored</u>

9 point lower case and UPPER CASE Helvetica italic and <u>underscored</u>

10 point lower case and UPPER CASE Helvetica plain and <u>underscored</u>

10 point lower case and UPPER CASE Helvetica bold and <u>underscored</u>
10 point lower case and UPPER CASE Helvetica italic and <u>underscored</u>

Such facilities are a great temptation to the new writer to make use of everything available. You should resist the temptation. If you use more than the necessary minimum of variation in a document, your document will look untidy and it will not be possible to tell what is more important from what is less important. Use this variety to help you plan a hierarchy of headings for your document, but don't overdo it.

A good hierarchy would be

MAIN HEADING CENTRED IN BOLD CAPITALS

1st level side headings in lower case bold

<u>2nd level side headings in lower case plain underscored</u>

3rd level side headings in lower case plain italic

Capitals

You should not be too free with the use of capitals for headings. Material printed in all capitals (upper case) is not as easy to read as the same material printed in upper and lower case letters. The reason for this is that we read more than just words when we read — we do part of our reading by recognising word shapes. If a line (or several lines) of words is presented in all capitals, their shapes are identical across the page, and we tend to skim over them because of this. On the other hand, if a line of words is presented in a mixture of initial capitals and lower case, the ascenders and descenders (the tops and tails) of letters like l, h, t and g, p, q help us to recognise the shapes of words. Contrast:

EFFECTIVE WRITING DOES THE TASK

Effective writing does the task   the

In this example, you can see the distinctive shapes made by the words printed in upper and lower case, compared with the lack of distinction of the top line of all capitals. Notice also the word **the**. Many little words like this one are so easy to recognise by the shapes they make that we hardly have to bother reading the letters.

If you have a computer that has decorative typefaces, be very careful in their use. They should not be used in most business documents at all. If you use them, take care to use them with discretion. Look at the two examples below and see how much better the second one makes its impact:

𝔐𝔢𝔯𝔯𝔶 𝔠𝔥𝔯𝔦𝔰𝔱𝔪𝔞𝔰 MERRY CHRISTMAS
Merry Christmas

Also remember your audience. If you are writing for an audience of 5-year-old children, have a look at the way children are taught to read and write. Reading material for little children uses *sans serif* types — that is, types that don't have a tiny cross stroke or ornament at the end of the main strokes of letters. Times is a serif type while Helvetica is sans serif:

Times: r n g
Helvetica: r n g

Notice the letter **g** in the serif type. Children learning to read have not met this curly **g**, so you should select a type that has the plain **g**. Older children, of course, can read both forms.

Signposts

Long documents such as formal reports, and even some short documents, can be made easier to read by providing the reader with signposts to show the way through the document. These signposts can take many forms. We have already looked at a suggestion for a hierarchy of headings based on type style. On most typewriters you have a choice of at least upper and lower case letters. You probably also have a choice of plain or bold.

Another signposting method is to use numbers or numbers and letters combined.

A First major part
  1 First sub-topic
  2 Second sub-topic
    (i) First sub-sub-topic
    (ii) Second sub-sub-topic
B Second major part

A Family (a)
  1 Genus (a)
  2 Genus (b)
    (i) Species (a)
    (ii) Species (b)
B Family (b)

The 'decimal' system of number is often used in formal reports. It is illustrated on page 149.

A third method of highlighting points or items in a list is to use dot points or bullets. Dot points are made with the full stop (.) and tend to be rather faint, whereas bullets (•) are made with a special device on the newer typewriters, word processors and computers, and show up very clearly. This method is used when the items do not need to be in any particular order.

Tables, diagrams, graphics etc

Often a table or graph will tell a story for you more simply than the equivalent prose. Which of the following do you find easier to comprehend at a glance — the text or the graphics?

(a) The shopping trolley survey for this week shows an interesting shift in shopping preferences as Christmas approaches. On average, shoppers spent 50 per cent of their budget on food, 20 per cent on personal items like underclothes and a massive 25 per cent on gifts. The rest was spent on plastic kitchenware. Last week, only 15 per cent of the budget was spent on gifts, with 25 per cent being spent on personal items and 10 per cent on kitchenware. Spending on food remained the same for the two weeks.

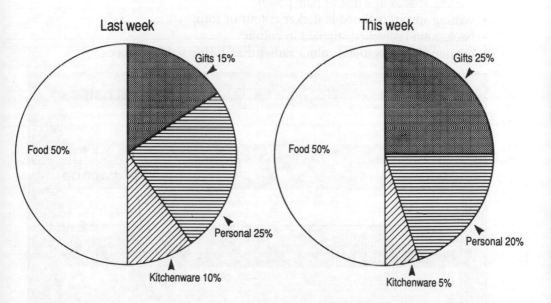

Pie charts if laid out well can convey facts and statistics efficiently and persuasively, and the information on them can be found quickly. They enhance writing by their appearance as well as by their function. Some of the graphic aids found on computers can help to show at a glance what the accompanying text is about, and even save the need to read it. But you should be careful not to overuse graphics. They should never be used to mask poor writing.

Packaging forms

We are all form-fillers, so we all have an interest in the design of forms. One of the problems with forms is that designers sometimes forget that there are many people to consider. As with all writing, the language and layout of a form will only be effective if it considers the whole audience. The users of a form include: the person who asked for it to be produced, the form-filler, the processor, the person who fills in the 'For Office Use Only' bits and the person who extracts the data from the form later — there may be more, but this will give you an idea of how many people are involved.

Form-fillers are probably the most important people to be considered in the language and layout of the form, because, if they don't get it right, everybody else along the line is affected. So the language of forms has to conform to all the principles of plain English that we have discussed in this book; in addition, spaces have to be the right size and placed so that the form-fillers can fill them in easily.

One of the most common tasks is filling in your name and address. A great deal of research has been done into the layout of this part of a form and the example below is typical of what the researchers believe is a satisfactory layout for most people to cope with. Its main points are:

- adequate vertical and horizontal space for writing
- writing spaces in white or pale pastel
- writing spaces outlined in darker colour of form
- background screened/stippled in colour
- captions in background colour rather than inside writing spaces

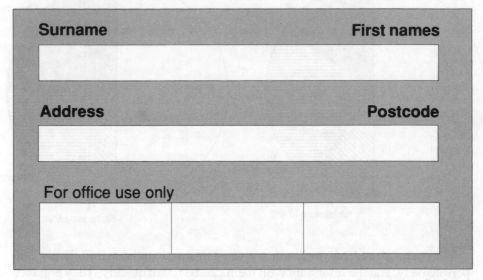

Well-designed forms are also consistent in their page layout — single or double column throughout, for instance. They also keep answer boxes in line with each other vertically, so that the form-filler's pen can move smoothly down the page and so that the form processor can pick up data easily.

As a writer, you are concerned with the language of forms. Here are some points about writing questions for forms which may help you:

1   Keep questions short and follow the principles of writing in a plain English style. Make sure that questions are capable of only one answer. Consider the form-filler — will he or she be able to remember the information you have asked for? Will it be relevant to the form-filler?

2   If you have to explain a question, put the explanation next to the question or it will probably not be read. People dislike filling in forms at the best of times, and they detest having to read booklets that attempt to guide them through the form or even having to turn the page over for the explanation. If you have to write a booklet of guidelines to help people complete a form (the leaflet V100 (see p 107) is an example), I suggest you consider the following points:

- Number points in the guidelines to match the numbers of the questions if they are meant to match each other. (If they are not, use letters of the alphabet.)
- Don't leave out any numbers — that is, if question 5 does not need a guideline, still put number 5 in the booklet but indicate that no guideline is necessary.
- Use the same clear typeface, typesize and colour scheme as the form.
- Use the clearest possible means of explaining difficult concepts — often the 'story' is the most satisfactory.

3   Keep questions in logical sequence. Sometimes you have to ask form-fillers to skip certain questions. Guide them to where they are supposed to go next by means of clear arrows. Make sure that, in doing so, you don't cause the form-filler to leave out essential questions.

4   Stick to one idea only in any question. Double-pronged questions are confusing and will produce inaccurate answers.

Exercises

Comment on these questions which are typical of many that appear on forms:

1   (From a primary school enrolment form) Hand? ....

2   (From a survey conducted by a firm which installs gas heating)

   Is your home unheated?   Yes ☐   No ☐

3   (From a questionnaire handed out outside a local cinema)

   How many times do you go to the cinema in a year?

   Often ☐   Sometimes ☐   Rarely ☐   Never ☐

4   Are you unmarried and in receipt of a pension? Answer YES or NO ————

Solutions

1   The question does not give enough information for the form-filler to answer adequately. A parent, when faced with such a question, might put TWO. Of course, the school should ask: Is your child mostly left-handed or right-handed?

2   This is a negative question. People do not think negatively, so a positive question would be easier for them to cope with. The risk here is that form-fillers will tick the YES box whether their homes are heated or unheated. A better question would be: Is your home heated?

3   This question will not get useful answers. The only answer that is not open to interpretation is 'never'. Such questions should be quantified. A better choice would be, for example:
   More than six times / Between three and six times / Between one and three times / Never.

4   This is a double-pronged question. How do you answer if you are married and get a pension, or unmarried and do not get a pension? Write two separate questions:
   Are you married? YES/NO   Are you in receipt of a pension? YES/NO

12 Writing plans

It would be a rare person indeed who could sit down and write a document of any length or complexity without planning it. In fact, nobody does. Even if some people seem to, they have really planned the document quite thoroughly in their heads. However, most of us have to make some notes, and how we organise our notes is the subject of this chapter.

There are many writing plans you can follow. You can make a **list** of things to write about, just as they occur to you. The trouble with that sort of plan is that it is never-ending. The list goes on and on, with nothing being organised into groups. The upshot is that you may write a document which rambles without ever getting anywhere.

You can decide on a **tree diagram**, like a genealogical tree, but the trouble with trees is that they grow. Not only do they grow branches, but twigs grow on the branches and leaves grow on the twigs. Trees also grow under the ground — roots spread and get tangled. It is very easy for a tree diagram to produce a document that goes off at tangents instead of sticking to the main thrust of the argument.

You may prefer a **pigeonhole** plan. With this plan, you write your ideas for different sections of the document on different sheets of paper and organise them as though you were sorting them into the pigeonholes of an old-fashioned desk. The trouble with this plan is that it is very difficult to keep ideas separated into what belongs in which pigeonhole. The result is some overlapping of information in pigeonholes and thus redundancy in the writing.

Another method is the **coathanger** plan, so called partly because of its triangular shape, and partly because you can hang coathangers on coathangers.

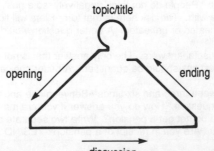

Under this plan, you think of your whole document as a coathanger with the topic or title of the document at the top. You mentally work down the left hand side of the shape with your opening remarks, across the bottom with your discussion, and up the right hand side with the ending, leading back to the title at the top. One advantage of this shape is that it is well defined — you are restricted to a definite triangular movement.

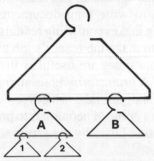

Another advantage is that you can hang little coathangers on the bottom of the main one, and still smaller ones from those. Each coathanger is the same shape, so the same planning procedure applies to each. You must finish dealing with one coathanger before you go on to the next, and you must finish with all the extra coathangers before you can write the ending to the whole document. In the diagram above, therefore, you must finish with the whole of items 1 and 2 before you can end sub-topic A and go on to sub-topic B. You must finish the whole of B before you can end the whole topic.

Suppose you want to write an advertising letter to sell a line of business briefcases to stationery stores. In your notes you might include:

Topic:
• Selling Briefcases (which may not eventually be your
  subject heading, of course).
Opening remarks:
• Name of line of briefcase:
    who needs one?
    what for?
Discussion :
• All about Sub-topic A including:
  1 features
  2 construction
  3 quality
• Sub-topic B — Money matters etc, including:
  1 price range
  2 availability
  3 how to order
  4 trade discounts
Ending
• Could include:
  1 early ordering for extra discount

2 free key case with each briefcase sold in promotion
   period
3 one free initialled leather notecase to manager of store
   ordering 20 or more briefcases
4 reiterate value and quality name

Follow any writing plan that appeals to you and works for you, but do follow one. It is not a good idea to write long documents, in particular, without planning. Unplanned writing makes confusing reading, and you should always remember that your task is to make the reader's job as easy as possible.

The only time that random notes are useful is in the very early stages of thinking about a document. A *brainstorming* session (where everyone present throws ideas into the ring, and you take whatever notes you think might be useful) can be valuable when a group of people has to produce a document. Ideas can be jotted down on a writing board by the group scribe and then sorted out according to a definite plan.

13 Documents, correspondence and report writing

We have looked at all the bits that go towards making up a complete document. Now we will look at some whole documents.

In a business situation, you may have to write many different documents in the course of a day or a week. Depending on your job, the documents you write will be routine minutes, letters and reports or they may include press releases, speeches and public information documents. We cannot include every possible document here, and we don't need to. The writing skills you have learned from reading everything in this book so far, particularly if you have been doing the exercises, will stand you in good stead for almost any document you want to write. There will still be documents that you need extra help with — 'specialist' documents like legal documents, forms, pamphlets and brochures — which require special thought and special design, but you can apply the principles of correct, plain English to all of them.

We will first of all run through a selection of the types of documents you may have to write.

File notes; electronic mail; messages

Perhaps you don't think of these as writing tasks. They are. They deserve every bit as much attention as any others. They all have to make sense to their addressees, and addressees are entitled to be able to understand them at first glance without having to ask questions.

File notes: These are for keeping a record of an interview with a business contact or of some change in a client's status. They are simply a handy way of updating a file, and should be brief— but not slangy. Use whole sentences.

Fax and Telex messages should be concise but should use complete sentences. Avoid jargon unless you know the recipient understands it, and be careful with some letters and figures which can easily become confused in transmittal. If there is any likelihood of confusion between the figure 1 and the small letter *l*, spell the figure out as ONE. Confusion between the figure 0 and the capital letter O can be avoided by using the zero with a line through it for the figure: Ø.

Note: Fax stands for facsimile. Therefore, you do not need to be quite so concise as in Telex messages, which are charged by the *number of characters* rather than by the page. It is important to note that handwritten fax messages are often very difficult to read, so typewritten messages are preferable.

Pitman Publishing

128 Long Acre
London WC2E 9AN

From 6 May 1990
Tel. 071-379 7383
Fax. 071-240 5771

Telephone 01-379 7383

Telex 261367
Pitman G

Cables Ipandsons
London WC2

Fax 01-240 5771
Pitman Ldn

FACSIMILE MESSAGE

To: L S James

From: Francis Hawkins

Date: 2 October 199-

Ref: ORDER FOR EFFECTIVE WRITING

No of pages: (including this one) 1

> Further to our telephone conversation this
> morning: I confirm that the 20 copies of
> EFFECTIVE WRITING were sent to you yesterday
> by special courier at 1145 hrs. Please
> notify us immediately if they have not been
> delivered by 1700 hrs today.

NOTE: IF YOU DO NOT RECEIVE ALL THE PAGES PLEASE PHONE OR TELEX US IMMEDIATELY ON THE ABOVE NUMBERS.

Pitman Publishing, Division of Longman Group UK Limited Registered Office 5 Bentinck Street London W1M 5RN Registered number 872828 England

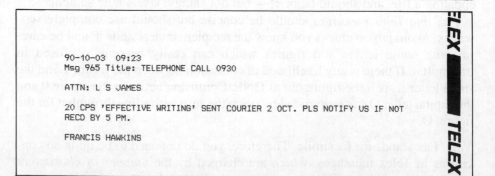

```
90-10-03  09:23
Msg 965 Title: TELEPHONE CALL 0930

ATTN: L S JAMES

20 CPS 'EFFECTIVE WRITING' SENT COURIER 2 OCT. PLS NOTIFY US IF NOT
RECD BY 5 PM.

FRANCIS HAWKINS
```

TELEX

TELEX

'While you were out' messages can be written like telegrams to save space but should still give complete information. Use the design of the form to help you — you can write half your message just by ticking the boxes provided. Then, in the space for the message, restrict yourself to what cannot be dealt with by ticking boxes. Handwriting is important on these forms — if there is not enough room for you to write clearly in your usual handwriting, type or print the message section on a sheet of paper and attach it to the form.

```
┌─────────────────────────────────────────────────────────────────┐
│  WHILE YOU WERE OUT              AM✓₁₂ PM                          │
│                                                                   │
│  ┌───────────────────┐                                            │
│  │     URGENT         │                                           │
│  ├─────────┬─────────┤           9 ◄─── 3                        │
│  │  NO✓    │  YES    │                                            │
│  └─────────┴─────────┘              6                             │
│  DATE  30/6                                                       │
│  TO   JIM ELLIS                                                   │
│  FROM  LEONIE JAMES          PHONE  x 635                         │
│  ① Wants you to attend Promotions meeting at                      │
│  2·30 tomorrow. I said you'd confirm. ② Don't                     │
│  forget lunch w. DG. TAKEN BY ____ E. M                           │
└─────────────────────────────────────────────────────────────────┘
```

Exercises

No solutions are provided for these Exercises — if you are part of a tutorial group, ask your tutor to assess your efforts for you. If you are working alone, ask a friend or your supervisor at work to assess them.

Write the appropriate documents for the following situations and audiences. Write no fewer than two and no more than four paragraphs, using sensibly-placed topic sentences and logical linking devices. Observe the basic rules of effective writing, including good grammar, correct spelling and correct sentence structure. Also observe the guidelines for writing in plain English.

Situation 1

You are working as assistant secretary in an architect's office. As a result of a meeting between your employer and a builder working on a house extension, the time schedules on the building work have now been changed. The floor covering cannot be laid until a week later than planned because of delivery delays.

Write an appropriate note to be put in the file entitled: 13 St Stephen's Road — extension works.

Situation 2

You have an appointment with your tutor to discuss some work. You now realise that you will be delayed by two hours because of a sudden emergency and you cannot reach them by telephone. Write a message that you could send by telex informing them of the situation.

Submissions

If you work in the public service, you may find yourself having to write submissions. These are documents which ask for approval of a policy or approval to do something. They vary in degree of formality from ordinary submissions which are put to your department head, right up to ministerial and cabinet submissions.

Whatever kind of submission you are writing, there are some things common to all of them. You must say what the submission is about and give the background to it. You should say what implications there would be (for example, financial, social, environmental), and what your recommendations are.

If your submission is straightforward and requires only a simple yes/no response, it is useful to provide a 'decision block' at the end which the approving officer merely has to complete. There is no need for that officer to write back to you in detail. Here is a suggestion that you can adapt to your own needs:

Proposal Approved / Not Approved
Signature _____
Title _____
Date _____

Minutes of a meeting

If you are responsible for taking the minutes of a meeting, don't worry that you don't do shorthand. It should not be necessary for most meetings. Meetings vary in importance and in degree of formality, so there are many variations on the standard methods of minute-recording. Indeed, for many meetings no record is kept at all.

For most meetings that keep records, all that is required word-for-word is any resolution voted on by those present, but you would be wise to keep a note of the names of the people who proposed and seconded motions, and the person who is to take action as a result of the resolution. Discussion leading up to the vote can be summarised unless somebody at the meeting specifically asks that a point be recorded word-for-word. Remember that you are merely the recorder — do not put your own interpretation on anything or include personal comment in the minutes. This is sometimes hard when you are both recorder and an active participant in the meeting.

The minutes are written up from your notes after the meeting. The completed document should show the purpose of the meeting, the date, time and place. It should give the names and titles of everyone present, noting who took the chair; in very large meetings, it may only be necessary to note the names of the committee members present, and add the number of others who were there. The minutes should summarise the views expressed in the meeting, show how each topic was dealt with and list the resolutions that were passed.

Minutes are normally written for members of your own organisation, so it is in order to use jargon terms if they best suit your purpose. Apart from this, minutes should be written in correct, plain English. Your colleagues above all, perhaps, will appreciate clear, flowing prose that they can absorb quickly and act on immediately.

BARNSTORMERS THEATRE CLUB
Minutes of a Meeting of the Committee of Management of the Barnstormers Theatre Club held at 5 Sunny Bank, Brinton Road, Cheltenham, Glos, GL23 7LD, on Saturday, 5 May 199- at 1700 hrs

Present: Joseph Bloggs   (Chairperson)
             Amy Smythe   (Vice-chairperson)
             David Webb   (Honorary Treasurer)
             James Harbinger
             Maurice Plinney
             Sonia Sprocket
             Joyce Stirling
             William Wilson
             Isobel Langley   (Secretary)

546   **Apologies:**
       Apologies were received from Adrian Cooper, Molly Entwhistle and Norman Hepworth.

547   **Minutes of the last meeting:**
       These were approved and signed.

548   **Matters arising:**
       Minute 545 Posters. The secretary reported that these had now been designed and the printing and distribution were in hand.

549   **Correspondence:**
       The secretary read a letter from The Little Theatre, Mickletop, confirming the telephone booking of 20 seats for the matinee performance of 'Arsenic and Old Lace' on Saturday, 17 July.

550   **Club premises:**
       Maurice Plinney reported that as yet he had been unsuccessful in his search for suitable premises for the Club. It was proposed by James Harbinger and seconded by Joyce Stirling that the possibility be explored of using the barn belonging to James Harbinger's father. The proposal was carried unanimously. James Harbinger volunteered to approach his father on the matter.

551   . . . .

When all the items on the Agenda have been dealt with, the date and the venue of the next meeting are decided and the Chairperson closes the meeting.

Press releases, articles for newspapers

Anything that you write for possible publication in the daily press is for a potentially very wide audience. You should bear in mind the average reading age of your audience, and keep your choice of words to those that all of your audience will understand. Sentences should be on the short side, but remember to vary the length a little to avoid the hypnotic effect of too many very short sentences.

Sub-editors have to fit news and articles into newspapers. Sometimes they cannot fit all of your story in, so they cut it. Normally they cut a story from the bottom up, so when you write a press release or an article, make sure that you tell the most important parts of your story in the first paragraph or two. Remaining paragraphs should cover further interesting aspects of the story, but should be progressively less important as the story goes on. It is most important in this kind of writing to remember what you learned about how paragraphs hold together. The whole story will collapse if you suddenly put in paragraph 5 something that refers to paragraph 1. Sub-editors tend to discard such poorly organised material altogether.

P R E S S   R E L E A S E

Issued by: DM Associates
           10 Grove Street
           Worcester   WS12 4NJ

12 September 199-   No 822/1
_____

NEW TRAINING UNIT FOR WORCESTER

A new training unit at City College is being opened
on 14 September at 10.30 am by Janet Seagrove, Mayor
of Worcester and former Principal of the College.

This will be an open-learning unit, supplying kit
courses in the latest engineering systems, language
and office skills, computers, catering, tourism and
management methods.

This system is also being used extensively by large
companies around Britain, and the new unit will
provide a major opportunity for employees of local
companies to brush up their skills.

This unit places Worcester in the forefront of quality
training in the UK - setting high standards to meet
the challenge of the new technologies.

- ends -

For further information and press pack contact
David Martin on 0905 2904994
                  Fax: 0905 2904885   Telex: 298512

Exercise (no solution provided)

Situation

You are walking along the High Street on your way to meet a friend. Suddenly a man, walking a few yards ahead of you, grabs a handbag from the basket of a woman looking in a shop window. He races off with it and you give chase. Fortunately the man is stopped by another passer-by and the police are sent for.

(a) Write the statement that you would make to the police.
(b) Write the story for the local newspaper.

Public information pamphlets/leaflets

These documents are only useful if they stick to one topic and cover it as concisely as possible. They are best if they contain illustrations, line drawings, cartoons, 'how-to' diagrams etc and if they use a friendly style. Chatty language works well, so you can afford to use slightly more colloquial language than you would use in a formal document. There is very little space on one of these documents and you have to plan carefully, remembering to include contact addresses and the source of the material. If you are writing a two-fold or three-fold pamphlet, plan what you will put on each panel and don't let material from one panel spill over into the next.

Be consistent in the format you adopt. *Question-and-answer* is usually good, if the questions are framed so that it appears as if the reader is asking them:

Q: Why do I have to vote?

A: Because it is the right of every Briton to......

Single-page leaflets give more scope for continuous writing, but are not as popular as pamphlets because they are not already folded into a convenient size.

However, they are useful for such things as gardening tips, where illustrations might take up more space than is available on one panel of a pamphlet. When printed on one side of the paper only, they can be pinned to a notice board and referred to when necessary.

Speeches

Writing a speech for someone else to deliver is quite a challenge. You must know the speaker's way of speaking very well so that you write the speech in the speaker's usual speaking style. Assuming you have this aspect under control, there are some more hurdles to overcome. You are writing for an audience of listeners instead of readers. Listeners cannot listen to something again in the way readers can re-read. Listeners do not have visible signposts to guide them through the speech in the way readers have headings, numbered paragraphs, highlighting and so on to guide them through a written document. You have to build all the signposting into the speech. Some tips that might help you are:

Tell them where you are going. Announce that you are going to talk about, say, three important points. Use sequencing devices like first, second, third, so that the listeners know exactly which point you have reached. If you start off with 'first' and then fail to announce the second and third points, your audience will be left waiting for the sequencing devices rather than listening to what the speaker has to say.

Tell them where you have been. At the end of, say, three points, do what radio announcers do — back announce them. Say something like 'Now that I've dealt with those three points, I'll go on to ....'.

Organise the speech into short chunks. People's short-term memory will hold only a small amount at a time. If you give listeners too much to take in at once, they will forget the first part before they have had time to process the whole idea. Organise the speech into an opening address (remembering to address the dignitaries according to protocol) and then a beginning, a developmental middle, and an end that draws the whole speech together.

Use repetition: Repetition of points you want people to remember is essential. In writing it can become boring, but listeners need to be reminded constantly of the important points.

Avoid unnecessary variation. Decide what word you want to use to describe a certain object or concept, and stick to it. If you are writing a speech on care of curtain fabrics, for example, decide whether you want to use the word *curtains* or *drapes* and stick to it, and make a choice between *fabrics* and *materials*, and so on. Unnecessary variation is confusing to listeners.

Use illustrations where necessary. If you want listeners to follow something complicated, consider providing handouts (but tell the listeners first if you are going to do this; otherwise they will go to the trouble of making their own notes). If you make overhead projector (OHP) transparencies to illustrate the main points of your talk, also say if you have handout copies of these. It is not a good idea to interrupt the speaker's flow by producing handouts at several points in the speech, so get all the illustrations on one piece of paper and hand it out at the beginning. Alternatively, if you do not want to risk having your audience concentrating more on a handout than on the speaker, consider preparing a handout of reminders for the audience to take away after the speech. If you think the audience could be confused about things like geographical locations, have a large map which the speaker can point to. The map must be large enough, and clear enough, to be seen easily from the back row of the audience. Don't let the speaker handle maps, blackboards, video equipment or even slide projectors and OHPs unless you are absolutely sure they will be handled expertly.

Know the audience. Find out who the audience will be and, as with writing, make sure that the speech will be pitched at the right level for them.

Correspondence and report writing

Minute or memorandum, and letter

In the public service the **memorandum** is the document you write to someone in another government department. In private organisations it is used when writing to anyone in the same organisation. They are much the same, except that the public service memorandum looks more like a letter, but without the inside address and close. The **minute** is used only in the public service, and is written to someone in your own section or department. Wherever you work, you write **letters** to people outside your own organisation.

Here is an example of a private sector memorandum:

ACME MANUFACTURING CO LTD
MEMORANDUM

To: Supervisor, Stores
From: T Pearson, storeman
Date: 15 June, 19--
Subject: Weekend Security of Stores

The workers in my section suggest that stricter security measures are needed to overcome pilfering during the weekends.

2 I agree with them that one security guard be transferred from regular duty to weekend duty to help the present guard.

3 I recommend that ID cards be required for access to stores.

TP

Here is an example of a typical public service minute setting out the same information:

Department of Office Services
MINUTE

90/1234

Supervisor, Stores

WEEKEND SECURITY OF STORES

The workers in my section suggest that stricter
security measures are needed to overcome pilfering
during weekends.

2 I agree with them that one security guard be
transferred from regular duty to weekend duty to
help the present guard.

3 I recommend that ID cards be required for access
to stores.

T Pearson
Storeman
     June 19—

Finally, here is a letter:

SECURITY SYSTEMS
123 SMIT STREET, LONDON NW4 5EA (081) 555 5432

20 June 199—

The Supervisor, Stores
Acme Manufacturing Co Ltd
PO Box 38
BROWNSVILLE BW2 5LA

Dear Sir

Thank you for your letter of 15 June.
My firm would be pleased to quote for
replacing your present security system.
I will be in Brownsville myself on Monday
next. May I call on you at 10 am? Please
telephone my secretary to confirm that this
arrangement will suit you.

Yours faithfully

I M Deadbolt

The structure of these documents is much the same; variations in layout are usually covered by in-house manuals. If your organisation does not have a manual, the layouts shown here are perfectly acceptable, and there are others in books such as *Model Business Letters* by L Gartside (Pitman) or *Pitman Business Correspondence* by G and D H Whitehead (Pitman).

Writing correspondence

The following remarks apply to all the documents we have just mentioned, but particularly to letters.

You know by now that paragraphs should stick to one subject at a time. The next step is to put the paragraphs together in a logical order. Here are some suggestions for structuring correspondence:

1 There must be an *opening section* of one or two paragraphs. This could be used for one or more of these purposes:

* to announce the topic;
* to give a reason for writing;
* to set the scene — that is, to put the document into its proper context and explain the background.

If it is a reply, the opening section could be used to refer to the reference document. In this case, there is no need to repeat the contents of the document you are replying to — just quote reference or folio numbers, date, subject heading, paragraph number etc.

If it is the start of fresh correspondence, the opening section could be used to introduce your organisation briefly. Then get on with it without further preamble. Remember your purpose in writing and stick to it.

2 Most of the rest of the document is *the message* (or *theme*). However many paragraphs you think you need, take care that you only write as many as are necessary to get your message across economically. This section of the document should:

* say what the topic is all about;
* say it in logically organised paragraphs;
* perhaps include evidence to back up statements or claims, reasons for requests, implications of proposals etc if necessary;
* perhaps include tables, graphs or statistics to illustrate an important point, interpreting them for the reader if they are capable of more than one interpretation.

3 The last part of the document is the *conclusion*. This could do one or more of the following: (a) sum up what has gone before; (b) emphasise the point you want the reader to remember most of all; and (c) say what action you want the reader to take.

The concluding part of correspondence should not take up more than two paragraphs — one to make your point, and one to end on a pleasant note if necessary. In most cases, the conclusion takes only one paragraph which combines these functions.

Here is an example of the body of a document which could be used as a memorandum or internal minute, or even as a letter to someone outside the organisation. Notice how the first paragraph introduces the topic, the second and third paragraphs say what it is all about (the second giving details and the third giving comment), and the fourth paragraph tells what action the reader should take. The language level and the sentence length are about right for the audience. The organisation of paragraphs is cohesive and logical. It ends when there is no more to say — no tacked-on courtesy here.

(Insert greeting etc as appropriate to document)

PLAIN ENGLISH AWARENESS SEMINAR

This confirms my phone call to you of this morning. Would it be possible for us to hold a seminar and lunch in your conference centre on Wednesday 23 February 19—? We expect between 70 and 80 participants, and this would be too many for us to accommodate in our own facilities. We would therefore appreciate your help again as you have helped us out before.

The seminar is entitled Plain English Awareness and will take all day, with breaks for morning and afternoon tea. There will be a lunch break of one hour when we plan to serve a light lunch in the reception area next to the conference room. Proceedings will start with registration at 8.30 am and end at 4.30 pm. If we may keep the rooms until 6 pm, we would like to be able to serve drinks after the seminar ends. Our staff will attend to all administrative details, including setting up the conference and reception rooms. We have engaged our usual caterer who will bring everything necessary for lunch and breaks.

We would be pleased if some of your senior staff could join us for this seminar. If past experience is anything to go on, it should be a valuable experience. There will be a number of well-known speakers addressing the group, and two of the morning sessions will be workshops. One of these workshops will give participants practical experience of writing in plain English. The other aims to give them experience of assessing written material from a plain English viewpoint. Our expert guests will be on hand all day to answer questions and help participants solve office writing problems they may have. I have attached a draft program which you are free to photocopy for your staff.

I would be grateful if you could confirm by the end of next week that you are able to accommodate us on 23 February. I will then be able to complete our plans and send details of the conference centre to participants. A phone call to me (ask for extension 1234) or to my secretary (ask for extension 1235) will suffice.

(Insert close as appropriate to document)

Exercises
No solutions are provided for these Exercises.

Situation 1

Apply to your immediate supervisor at work for permission to attend a course on Effective Writing to be held in your organisation soon (invent any details you need).

Situation 2

For your supervisor's signature, write to the consultant who ran the course in Situation 1 to thank him/her on behalf of the participants from your department.

Situation 3

On behalf of your supervisor, write to the director of staff development of a government department other than your own, or of another organisation, inviting him/her to attend a seminar in your department which will be of mutual interest and benefit.

Situation 4

You have recently returned from a posting in Sydney. A suitcase has gone astray and has been missing for a week now. You have already brought the matter to the attention of the appropriate authorities verbally. Now do the following:

(a) Write to the airline concerned, giving full details of flight, description of suitcase and contents, where you last saw it, details of insurance, and anything else you think the airline should be told, including what you want done.

(b) Write to the Sydney representative of the department or organisation which arranged the transport of your luggage, indicating what you have done so far and asking that appropriate enquiries be made from Sydney as well about your missing suitcase.

(c) Write to the officer responsible for staff travel in your department or organisation pointing out that you are not satisfied with the service you have received from this airline and requesting that travel to your next posting (to New York in a few weeks' time) be with another reputable airline.

Situation 5

You have no sooner posted documents (a), (b) and (c) in Situation 4 than your suitcase turns up, delivered in person by a senior executive of the airline, who could not be more apologetic. It seems it was wrongly identified by another passenger on your flight as hers, and she did not notice the error until she tried to unlock it. Her suitcase was waiting for her at the airline's office.

Write whatever follow-up documents you think necessary.

Situation 6

Write to a recent applicant for a position in your section telling them (1) that they have been successful and should report for work next Monday; (2) that they have been unsuccessful. (Try to be encouraging).

Job applications

At some time, most people who want a job have to apply in writing. Your job application could be the most important document you ever write, and it therefore deserves care. We will first look at an example of a job advertisement for the public service and a letter replying to the advertisement.

DEPARTMENT OF
ADMINISTRATION OF OTHER DEPARTMENTS
DUMFRIES
Administrative Service Officer
CLASS 2 — £ 12 850 – £15 230

Applications are invited for the above position from suitably qualified persons.

The position is located in the The West Wing, County Hall, Dumfries. The successful applicant will prepare pamphlets for distribution to the public on the functions of the Department; proof-read and correct proofs of pamphlet reprints including, when necessary, using a visual display terminal. The appointee will also provide general clerical assistance to the Director-General as directed.

Further information, duty statement and selection criteria
may be obtained by phoning Ms J Priatel (062) 111 2345. Selection will be made on the basis of the selection criteria. It is in the interests of candidates to obtain the selection criteria and frame their applications accordingly.

Conditions of service
include four weeks annual leave plus leave bonus, cumulative sick leave, three months long service leave after ten years service and a comprehensive superannuation scheme. To be eligible for appointment, applicants must be British citizens.

Applications, showing full particulars of qualifications and experience, together with a contact telephone number and address, should be forwarded to:

The Recruitment Officer
Department of Administration of Other Departments
COUNTY HALL
DUMFRIES DF1 2BY
by 31 December 19—

AN EQUAL OPPORTUNITY EMPLOYER
Nobody smokes in our offices; we have a separate smoke room/coffee shop for staff.

Job advertisements these days give only some of the details of the job. You are expected to phone the organisation concerned to ask for the job description and selection criteria for the job. ('Selection criteria' means the standards by which applicants will be judged for the position. I have not shown actual selection criteria in this example because they are normally set out on forms and would take up too much space.) Read the advertisement carefully to find out what you should do and address yourself to the selection criteria in your application.

Dear Sirs

I wish to apply for the position of
Administrative Service Officer, Class 2,
which was advertised in 'The Glasgow Times'
on Saturday, 19 June.

As you can see from the enclosed CV, I have
had considerable experience in writing for
a general readership, and so I believe that
I am well qualified to write pamphlets for
public distribution.

My standards of spelling and grammar are
high. I gained first prize for English at
College, and my typing is accurate at 75
words a minute (see enclosures).

Although I enjoy working in a team, I am
perfectly happy working on my own, and I
have a good level of concentration.

You will find all details of my education,
business training and work experience on the
enclosed CV, together with the names and
addresses of my referees.

I believe that I meet the selection criteria
and hope that I may be considered a suitable
applicant for this position. I can be
contacted during business hours on 111 5432,
and I am available for interview at any time
convenient to you.

Yours faithfully

The reply to this advertisement would begin with an opening paragraph which sets out what job you are applying for and where you saw it advertised. Your second paragraph is where you 'sell' yourself — that is, you say why you think you are well qualified for the position and why you want it. Most of the remaining paragraphs should cover, one paragraph at a time, all the selection criteria set out by the employer. Do not leave any of them out. Your final paragraph should say how you can be contacted for an interview and should end on a pleasant note.

Our next example is a letter applying for a job which had no formal selection criteria. In this sort of letter, you should extract what you can from the advertisement, addressing yourself to the points made in it.

On page 143 is a CV (summary or résumé) of personal details, qualifications and experience. CV stands for curriculum vitae (Latin for 'life history') and is the title most commonly used in this country. There are many ways of setting out a CV — this example follows a traditional pattern. You should always rewrite your CV for each job you apply for so that it applies to the particular position. I have shown only one CV, but of course a CV should accompany every application.

```
Dear.........

Please consider me for the position of Staff
Development Officer (..............).

My experience includes two years as a training
officer in  ...... where I helped to plan and
conduct courses in communication skills.  My
present position in  ...... has given me expe-
rience of the administrative side of staff
training and development.  It has involved or-
ganising study assistance for staff members and
researching the graduate and undergraduate
studies available in the tertiary institutions
in Glasgow.

I recently attended a course on writing in
plain English, and I would like an opportunity
to pass on what I have learned to others.

A copy of my curriculum vitae is enclosed, with
the names and addresses of three referees whom
you may contact.  I look forward to an inter-
view at any time convenient to you.  You may
phone me at work on 222 3333.

Yours sincerely
```

Report writing

Reports are part of business life. We report to other people so that they will have information on which they can base the decisions they have to make. Reports can consist of just a few lines written as a memorandum or minute; or they can be long, formal documents of several pages or even several volumes. They can stand alone, as most short memo reports can, or they may need a transmittal document to go with them — letter, memorandum or minute. They are not the writing bogey that some people make them out to be. If you can write paragraphs, you can write reports.

CURRICULUM VITAE

Name:	Sandra Patel
Address:	113 London Road, Manchester, MC2 4SW
Telephone:	Work 061–222 3333 Home 061–285 9394
Date of birth:	1 December 19--
Nationality:	British
Status:	Single

Education

School:	Westcliffe High School, Priory Road, Bolton

Qualifications:

GCSE	**grade**
English language	B
English literature	C
Mathematics	A
Science	A
French	B

Other achievements:	School prefect
	School netball team captain
	Member of the school swimming team

College:	Thornton College of Further Education
	Thornton, TH5 3NJ

Qualifications:

'A' level	**grade**
English literature	B
Biology	B
Economics	C

Higher education:	Liverpool Polytechnic
Qualifications:	BA (English and Psychology)

Work experience

19-- to 19--	Training officer with Department of . . .
	Duties included:
	Helping to plan courses in communication skills for junior clerical officers
	Helping the senior training officer to organise symposiums for senior and middle management
	Conducting courses in basic English for word processor operators
19-- to present	Personnel Officer with Department of . . .
	Duties include:
	Staff development and training
	Preparing leaflets and guidelines
	Assisting with and conducting induction courses
Personal interests:	Competition netball and swimming, entertaining, collecting early rock records and writing poetry

Referees:

Ms A Nover	Prof Henry Higgins	Mr Peter Savoy
Staff Development Officer	Department of Psychology	113 King's Crescent
Department of . . .	Liverpool Polytechnic	Manchester
Government Buildings	Rodney House	M13 5PY
City Road	Mount Pleasant	
Wolverhampton	Liverpool	
WL5 8RY	L3 5UX	

Short memorandum reports

In this section, we will look at some examples of short memorandum reports.

Reports can be classified in various ways, but here we will stick to one classification — by function: informational, interpretative or analytical.

An **informational report** gives the facts only. It does not interpret figures or comment on them in any way. Most periodic reports are purely informational — it is left to the person who asked for the report to do any interpreting and draw conclusions.

Here is an example of an informational report. It is set out here as an internal memorandum. It could equally well be set out as a minute or as a letter from a consultant to a client.

TO: Sales Manager

FROM: Jo Bourke, Senior Sales Representative,
           Midland Region

DATE: 12 December 19—

SUBJECT: Sales for November 19—

Here are the sales figures for last month in my area.

My Midland Region colleagues, Brad Graham and Pam Gibson, and I made 248 visits during November. A total of 102 sales resulted from these visits, and the amount of sales was £21 810.

The sales breakdown is as follows:

	Visits	Sales	Amount
Supermarkets	36	36	£6 599
Pharmacies	30	30	6 200
Hardware stores	42	22	5 800
Clothing stores	60	6	1 223
Banks and building societies	55	5	1 010
Miscellaneous small businesses	25	3	978
Totals:	248	102	£21 810

JB

An **interpretative report** gives the facts and interprets them for the reader. For example, if the facts include figures, the figures may be interpreted as percentages by the report writer. These reports are useful for setting out technical data in a form that a non-technical person can understand. Without the interpretation, the reader may not understand the significance of figures presented in a purely informational report — or may misinterpret them.

Here is an example of an interpretative report. It is the same report as the one above, expanded to interpret the figures for the reader.

TO: Sales Manager

FROM: Jo Bourke, Senior Sales Representative,
            Midland Region

DATE: 12 December 19—

SUBJECT: Sales for November 19—

Here are the sales figures for last month in my area.

My Midland Region colleagues, Brad Graham and Pam Gibson, and I made 248 visits during November. A total of 102 sales resulted from these visits, and the amount of sales was £21 810.

The sales breakdown is as follows:

	Visits	Sales	Amount
Supermarkets	36	36	£6 599
Pharmacies	30	30	6 200
Hardware stores	42	22	5 800
Clothing stores	60	6	1 223
Banks and building societies	55	5	1 010
Miscellaneous small businesses	25	3	978
Totals:	248	102	£21 810

The figures show that supermarkets, pharmacies and hardware stores account for 85 per cent of the sales although they constitute less than half (43.5 per cent) of the visits.

JB

An **analytical report** gives the facts and interprets them and goes one step further. It comments on the facts, interpreting them by suggesting reasons for them and explaining their significance. It also draws conclusions and makes recommendations based on the facts. It is important for you to know whether or not you are to write an analytical report — to do so without being told may be thought of as presumptuous, while to fail to do so when it is expected may be regarded as carelessness on the part of the writer. Always make sure what kind of report is required.

Here is an example of an analytical report. It is the same as the interpretative report above, expanded to include analysis of the information and recommendations.

```
TO:        Sales Manager
FROM:      Jo Bourke, Senior Sales Representative,
           Midland Region
DATE:      12 December 19—
SUBJECT:   Sales for November 19—

Here are the sales figures for last month in my
area.

My Midland Region colleagues, Brad Graham and
Pam Gibson, and I made 248 visits during November.
A total of 102 sales resulted from these visits,
and the amount of sales was £21 810.

The sales breakdown is as follows:

                                 Visits    Sales    Amount
Supermarkets                       36        36     £6 599
Pharmacies                         30        30      6 200
Hardware stores                    42        22      5 800
Clothing stores                    60         6      1 223
Banks and building societies       55         5      1 010
Miscellaneous small businesses     25         3        978
                                  ___       ___    _____
                Totals:           248       102    £21 810
```

The figures show that supermarkets, pharmacies and hardware stores account for 85 per cent of the sales although they constitute less than half (43.5 per cent) of the visits.

I believe that the reason supermarkets, pharmacies and hardware stores account for the bulk of the sales is that they have linoleum, cork or concrete floors which require more of our industrial cleaners than the others do. The other businesses generally have carpeted floors.

I recommend that we concentrate sales visits in future on supermarkets, pharmacies and hardware stores. Sales staff should call on other businesses only once every three months, or as time permits.

JB

Whatever type of report you are writing, observe the conventions of correct grammar and plain English. Here is an organising timetable you can follow for writing any report. Such a timetable is more important if you are writing a long, formal report than if you are writing a short, memo report.

1 Define the scope.
  • Make sure you clarify this with the person who asks for the report.
  • Define it for yourself by writing down a working title.
2 Gather information
  • from primary sources such as:
    direct observation
    experiment — perhaps a survey of types of equipment, products or services
    interviews
    written questionnaires
  • from secondary sources (for back-up only):
    library references
    office files dealing with similar situations.
3 Collate information
  • discarding any that turns out to be irrelevant or duplicated
  • highlighting important information
  • clarifying any contradictions of facts.
4 Prepare a writing plan.
  (See suggestions in chapter 12.)
5 Write a draft.
  • Do it quickly. At this stage do not worry too much about grammar or style; it is better to get points down, even in note form, than to try to polish as you write.
  • Include everything that is necessary to the final report. Check back to make sure that the content matches the requirements of your brief and the scope of the report.
  • Get a colleague to check for facts and total content — two heads are better than one here. Don't throw out your raw data until you are certain you don't need them any more.
6 Write the final report:
  • editing and polishing language and style
  • following an established layout for ease of reading and indexing.

Exercises (no solutions provided)

1 Informational report:
  Report to your immediate supervisor at work on aspects of a course you have attended recently (or the course you are currently attending). Include such details as:
  a numbers attending <u>and</u> departments/sections represented (use a table);
  b course content — Day 1, Day 2 etc.

2 Interpretative report:
Expand the informational report to include:
a your interpretation of the table — for example, what proportion of staff in each department or section is represented by these figures;
b your interpretation of the course content as far as it has been covered — that is, what you now understand by each of the headings you have used in the course content part of the informational report.

3 Analytical report:
Expand the interpretative report to include:
a your and other participants' views on the usefulness or otherwise of various items included in the course program (be objective);
b your recommendations (based on the above) for changes in the course program, if any (be constructive).

Longer reports

There are several acceptable layouts for longer *formal reports*. This is a common one:

- Covering minute/memorandum or letter (transmittal document) — with long reports only
- Summary including background to the report, plus recommendations (applicable with very long reports)
- The report proper in logical sequence (see suggested sequence accompanying the formal report exercise below), complete with diagrams, statistics etc.
- Conclusions (and recommendations if not included in a summary)
- Appendices (charts, extra statistics etc, references, acknowledgements).

We will illustrate a formal report by means of the example below. (You may like to use it as an exercise to work through.)

Exercise (no solutions provided)

Formal report — briefing

Last week there was a small fire in one of the syndicate rooms in the training section of your building. Someone had thrown a lighted match into a wastepaper bin and it caught alight. As the bin was quite close to curtains, it was fortunate that a passing course participant smelt the burning material and put the fire out by smothering it with a handy telephone book before taking the whole bin to the kitchen and pouring water into it. This experience has alerted management to the need for a review of fire prevention facilities.

You are to research and write up a short formal report on this fictional situation. Concentrate only on those parts of the building to which course participants have access — nowhere else inside the building.

Aspects you might consider examining could include some of these:

- construction of the building, internal and external (if relevant, and if they can be examined);

- surrounding environment (if relevant);
- furnishing materials, flammable materials etc;
- escape routes in the event of fire (there are sometimes up to 40 people in the main conference room);
- corridors, conference and syndicate rooms, kitchen, toilets — ease of exit etc;
- current sprinkler and/or fire extinguisher systems;
- warning signs, exit markers, smoking/no-smoking practices/signs, drills, etc.

Arrive at conclusions based on your findings — do not make unfounded statements. Then make recommendations based on your conclusions. Recommend nothing that you cannot back up by having first drawn conclusions from actual findings.

Regard the report as urgent. You should be able to complete it (investigation, draft and final report) in about two hours. If you are working in a group, you could team up with one other person.

When you finish the report, put your name(s) and designations at the end, together with the date.

Formal report — sequencing

There are several acceptable ways of sequencing the body of the report. Here is one which you can follow for most formal reports, including this exercise.

Title:	REPORT ON .... (in capitals)
1. *Terms of reference*:	**1.** On the instructions of .... on Memo/Minute .... of ....
2. *Procedure*:	**2.1** What you did first (eg inspection)
	2.2 What you did next (eg interviews) .... and so on
3. *Findings*:	**3.1** Building construction
	3.1.1 External
	3.1.2 Internal .... and so on
	3.2 Surrounding environment .... and so on
4. *Conclusions*:	**4.1** ...... etc (may be numbered or just one logical paragraph)
5. *Recommendations*:	**5.1** That the outside of the building ....
	5.2 That fire drills .... and so on (based on your own findings)
Reporting officer/s:	Name/s and titles at end of report
Date:	Date of report

This sequencing plan is self-explanatory. Note the numbering system: it is helpful to the reader if you number sections in some way, and this 'decimal' system is widely accepted in business and in the public service. It also helps if, along with numbers, you use side headings throughout the report. Together, they act as excellent signposts to guide the reader's eye to the sections that are of particular interest. Here is a sample of how this might appear:

3 FINDINGS

3.1 <u>Building construction</u>

3.1.1 *External*
    We found that the external walls of the building were made of
        weatherboard material.

3.1.2 *Internal*
    The internal walls were made of plasterboard and wood.

Do not extend the numbering to more than three 'decimal' points (as 3.1.2.1); this is the most that average readers can manage without becoming confused.

If it is required for a long report, here is an outline of what you should include in a summary of the report. This is placed at the beginning of the report proper.

SUMMARY OF REPORT ON .... (in capitals)

1. XXX (author/s) recommend/s that...... (recommendation/s first)

2. These recommendations are based on the fact that ....

3. I/we expect that the provision of ... would ... (desirable outcome).

Transmittal document

The transmittal document that goes with a formal report is a letter, memo or minute officially sending the report to the person(s) who requested it. Your transmittal document should include:

1 The transmittal itself;

2 An overview of the report;

3 Acknowledgement to anyone who helped you prepare the report — staff, other course participants, and any other sources of assistance;

4 A courteous close — here you could do any or all of the following:
  a say what you think should happen next (further investigation, discussion with others etc),
  b express your pleasure at having been asked to make the report,
  c indicate that you are willing to elaborate on points in the report in person if required.

On the next page is a sample transmittal document (not related to the report in the exercise above).

```
APPROPRIATE HEAD (letter, memo, etc)

Date

Addressee and address


Dear Mr Jackson

  Here is the report you asked for on 23 August analys-
ing the problems that exist in the training section.

  Briefly, the report sets out the problems we dis-
cussed in our meeting of 23 August, together with what
I discovered during my investigation.  I have inter-
preted these findings for you in terms that management
can relate to.  My analysis of the situation includes
possible causes of the problems.  I have made specific
recommendations about how they might be solved both in
the short term and over a period of three years.

  I would be glad to discuss with you any questions you
may have about the report.  I strongly urge that you
put my short term recommendations into effect immedi-
ately so that the current ill-feeling in the training
section can be remedied promptly.

Yours sincerely


Ann Bradley
Staff Relations Officer
```

Exercise (no solution provided)

Write a transmittal document to go with the report on page 148–9.

14 Conclusion

A document only works if it can be seen to work. To see if it works, you must *test* it in the field. Some documents, such as forms, need a great deal of testing to find out which parts work well with their audience and which do not. Each testing session is followed by amendments and further testing. Some documents, such as minutes, may need only a quick check by a colleague.

Even something as apparently simple as a public information leaflet needs *reviewing* on a regular basis to make sure that it still says what you want it to say. There is nothing as stale as a stale pamphlet — keep information up to date, check for changes in technology, and very importantly, make sure that the language of the document reflects the spoken language of the day.

Everyday working documents such as minutes, memorandums, letters and reports need to be considered carefully before they are sent to their readers. If any one of the conventions of acceptable grammar or of plain English is not upheld, the document will not be completely effective. *Rewriting* for effectiveness is part of writing.

Now that you have reached the end of this book, you have worked through a lot of exercises on points of grammar and plain English. You have applied these points to writing paragraphs and you have put paragraphs together to form effective documents. The rest is up to you. No document should hold any terrors for you ever again. You will certainly have to find out for yourself how to set out documents that are strange to you, but that is merely a matter of consulting your office manual. You can approach any writing task now with confidence that your grammar will be acceptable and that your style of writing will be easy to read. You will be more aware now of what makes your own and others' writing effective.